THE FORTIFICATI
MALTA
1530–1945
FROM THE KNIGHTS OF MALTA TO BRITISH RULE

Charles Stephenson · Illustrated by Steve Noon

This edition published in 2004 in association with Progress Press Co. Ltd., a member of the Allied Group.

First published in Great Britain in 2004 as Fortress 16: The Fortifications of Malta 1530–1945 by Osprey Publishing, Elms Court, Chapel Way, Botley, Oxford OX2 9LP, United Kingdom.
Email: info@ospreypublishing.com

ISBN 1 84176 836 7

Editorial by Ilios Publishing, Oxford, UK (www.iliospublishing.com)
Maps by The Map Studio, Romsey, UK
Index by Alison Worthington
Design: Ken Vail Graphic Design, Cambridge, UK
Originated by Grasmere Digital Imaging, Leeds, UK
Printed and bound by L-Rex Printing Company Ltd.

04 05 06 07 08   10 9 8 7 6 5 4 3 2 1

A CIP catalogue record for this book is available from the British Library.

FOR A CATALOGUE OF ALL BOOKS PUBLISHED BY OSPREY MILITARY AND AVIATION PLEASE CONTACT:

Osprey Direct UK, PO Box 140, Wellingborough, Northants, NN8 2FA, UK
Email: info@ospreydirect.co.uk

Osprey Direct USA, c/o MBI Publishing, PO Box 1, 729 Prospect Ave, Osceola, WI 54020, USA.
Email: info@ospreydirectusa.com

www.ospreypublishing.com

Artist's note

Readers may care to note that the original paintings from which the colour plates in this book were prepared are available for private sale. The Publishers retain all reproduction copyright whatsoever. All enquiries should be addressed to:

Steve Noon
50 Colchester Avenue
Penylan
Cardiff
CF23 9BP
UK

The Publishers regret that they can enter into no correspondence upon this matter.

Dedication

To the people of the Republic of Malta, who for far too long were players in other people's history.

Acknowledgements

In writing this book I am glad to acknowledge the contribution made to it by several others. It is commonplace, though true, to say that without their assistance it would not have been possible for it to be written. In the UK I owe thanks to Mr Kevin Ryan, Mr Iain Stewart and, in particular, Mrs Pamela Stephenson. From the Republic of Malta I would like to thank Mr Wilfrid Asciak, Mr Ray Cachia-Zammit, Mr Joe Sammut, Mr Ian Ellis, and Mr Stephen C Spiteri. It is actually impossible to write about the Maltese fortifications without acknowledging the debt owed to Stephen Spiteri. His extensive research over many years has created the quarry from which the rest of us must take our stone. Though they have all been of great assistance, it goes almost without saying that any errors herewith are mine and mine alone.

Contents

Introduction

Malta has one of the highest concentrations of military works anywhere in the world and it is the purpose of this book to attempt to address and explain why such a physically small part of the world should have been so coveted, for the presence of such extensive defences implies powerful enemies to defend against. Though this book is about the fortifications of Malta and not the political or military history of the island, it is obvious that to ignore the context within which such fortification took place would be to imply that it occurred in a vacuum. The rich, one might say unparalleled, military-archaeological heritage evident on the Maltese archipelago did not spring up unbidden.

It sprang from the geographical fact that the island of Malta possesses, in those harbours now known as Grand and Marsamxett, two of the finest anchorages in the world. It was the existence of these, combined with the location of the island, which made Malta a strategically vital point for more than four centuries. Vital because, at different times, it sat athwart the lines of communication of three mighty empires.

The first empire to feel the pressure on its communications was that of the Ottomans, and in order to slacken the pressure a mighty, though unsuccessful, campaign was launched. There was no guarantee that having failed once another, greater, attempt might be made and to deter this potential threat the island was equipped with a vast array of defensive works. This work will deal with what was constructed, what it was meant to achieve and the principles that drove it to be constructed in the manner that it was.

Malta became both a part of the British Empire and a vital link in its communication network. Technological and political changes rendered the older fortifications obsolete and the British fortified the island with updated structures and methods. Again what was constructed, where it was placed and what it was meant to achieve will be considered.

The third imperial power to focus attention on Malta was Italy; *mare nostrum* being little more than an aspiration whilst Malta sat athwart the sea routes to the Italians' North African possessions. Once again technological advances changed the nature of fortification and these changes, and what they meant to the defenders and fortifiers of Malta, are explored.

Because of the geo-political factors mentioned above, it is possible to trace the history of fortification from the 16th to the 20th century on this one small island. There may be other places where so great a range can be studied in such a small area, but if so I do not know of them. In short, if one were to conceive of an exhibit to display the history of the science of European fortification, one would come up with something rather like Malta.

Chronology

1522	The Knights of St John are forced to evacuate Rhodes after the successful Ottoman siege

Malta Under The Knights Hospitaller – 1530–1798

1530	The Knights arrive in Malta and Tripoli
1541	Annexation of Hungary by the Ottoman Empire
1551	Large-scale Ottoman raid carries off the population of Gozo. Tripoli taken
1565	The Great Siege. Decision taken to construct what became the city of Valletta.
1570–71	The Ottomans capture Cyprus
1571	Valletta becomes the Knights' new capital. The battle of Lepanto destroys the Ottoman fleet
1588	The Spanish Armada, a key anti-Ottoman force, thwarted by Drake and destroyed by weather
1609	Beginning of the first phase of construction of coastal towers
1618	End of first phase of construction of coastal towers
1635	Construction of Floriana and Sta Magherita Lines begun
1636	Beginning of second phase of construction of coastal towers
1657	End of second phase of construction of coastal towers
1658	Beginning of third phase of construction of coastal towers
1667	End of third phase of construction of coastal towers
1670	Cottonera Lines commissioned. Decision taken to construct Fort Ricasoli. Candia (Crete) falls to the Ottoman Empire
1715	Construction of coastal batteries and redoubts begun
1723	Work begins on Fort Manoel. Inland and coastal entrenchments constructed
1773	Cessation of work on entrenchments
1789	The French Revolution
1792	Fort Tigne started. Cessation of construction of coastal batteries and redoubts
1798	The French under Napoleon Bonaparte invade and take Malta en route to Egypt. The Maltese population rises against their new masters and blockade them in Valletta

British Imperial Malta – 1800–1939

1800	The French capitulate to the British. The United States of America launches a naval and military campaign against the North African corsairs
1804	US forces capture the North African city of Darna and sign a treaty with the corsairs
1815	Malta proclaimed a British Crown Colony
1820–30	The Knights' coastal defences abandoned by the British as too weak
1837	The French introduce shell-firing guns into their inventory
1849	The construction of St Clement's retrenchment begun
1884	Lascaris Battery, within Grand Harbour, constructed
1859–60	Rationalisation of ordnance undertaken
1842	Rifled Muzzle Loading (RML) artillery makes its debut
1858	The French Navy launches *La Gloire*, the first seagoing ironclad vessel.
1859	The British counter *La Gloire* with HMS *Warrior*, the first vessel built entirely of iron
1860	The Royal Commission into the defence of Britain recommends that extensive works of fortification be undertaken. New construction of fortifications to defend Malta recommended. Unified Italian Navy created

1869	Italian Navy suffers a heavy defeat at the hands of the Austro-Hungarian fleet at the battle of Lissa
1872	Fort Sliema constructed
1874	Fort St Lucien constructed
1875	Forts Pembroke and St Leonardo begun. Work begins on defensive positions on the Great Fault
1876	Fort Delimara constructed
1878	Cambridge Battery and Fort Madalena begun
1879	Fort Tas Silg and Rinella Battery begun
1880	Fort Mosta begun
1881	St Paul's Battery begun
1882	Zonqor Battery constructed
1889	Spinola, Del Grazie and Garden Batteries constructed
1897	Wolseley and Pembroke Batteries constructed. The Victoria Lines, named in honour of Queen Victoria's Diamond Jubilee, commissioned
1910	Fort Benghisa begun
1911–12	Italy takes possession of Libya from the Ottoman Empire
1914–18	World War I. Malta a vital British base, but thanks to the Italian decision not to join with Germany and Austria-Hungary, not subject to direct attack from the Central Powers. The rise of air power during the war renders Malta open to potential attack from Italy
1922	The Fascists seize power in Italy. Mussolini considers modern Italy to be the inheritor of the Roman Empire and adopts expansionist rhetoric. The position of Malta seems somewhat incongruous with the notion of *mare nostrum*.
1934	Acoustical mirror, 'Il Widna', constructed in an attempt to counter the threat posed by Italian aircraft
1935–36	Italo–Abyssinian War. The Italians conquer Abyssinia with the aid of air-delivered mustard gas

World War II and beyond – 1939–2003

1939	World War II erupts in mainland Europe. The first radar set to be deployed outside the UK is sent to Malta
1940	Defeat of France and removal of the French Fleet from the Mediterranean. Italy declares war and attacks Malta from the air. Air and naval forces from Malta interdict Axis supply lines to North Africa. The beginning of the Second Siege
1942	Operation Herkules, the Axis plan for the invasion of Malta, is planned, but never put into operation. Malta awarded the George Cross
1943	Italy invaded by Allied forces and capitulates. Italian Battle Fleet sent to Malta
1945	Germany surrenders to the United Nations
1964	Malta becomes independent within the British Commonwealth
1974	Malta leaves the Commonwealth and becomes a Republic
2003	Malta votes to join the European Union

Malta under the Knights Hospitaller – 1530–1798

'St Elmo is the key to Malta,' pronounced Jean Parisot de la Valette, Grand Master of the Knights of St John from 1557 to 1568, in the year 1565, the year of the Great Siege by the forces of the Ottoman Turks. Fort St Elmo lay at the tip of the peninsula of Mount Sciberras, upon which was later constructed the fortified city named after Valette, and his appraisal was both correct in the context he made it and also of value from the strategic perspective.

The Maltese archipelago, and more particularly the main island of Malta itself, occupies a vital strategic position in the Mediterranean Sea. It is so situated in the narrows between Europe to the north and Africa to the south so as to be the key position that can control communication between the western and eastern Mediterranean. This position is further enhanced by the two excellent harbours found on the east coast, Marsamxett and Grand Harbour; the latter amongst the finest natural harbours on the globe. Whoever possesses these harbours can decide who passes from one end of the Mediterranean to the other. Valette's aphorism might almost be enlarged upon to argue that St Elmo was the key to strategic control of the central Mediterranean.

This requires qualification however, because St Elmo, though of vital importance in the defensive scheme, was not necessarily alone and of itself the key to Grand and Marsamxett harbours. A glance at the map of the harbour area immediately conveys the crucial importance of the fortifications located on the peninsulas of Senglea (Fort St Michael) and Birgu (Fort St Angelo), and the fortified walls to the south. Whoever held these positions could exercise control over Grand Harbour, whereas possession of St Elmo alone could only deny control rather than exercise it. Strategically then, the construction of all subsequent fortifications on Malta had as their fundamental purpose the protection of the vitally important harbour area, with perhaps two exceptions: the city of Mdina and the island of Gozo.

The Maltese archipelago and Ottoman communications. The island of Malta possesses in those harbours now known as Grand and Marsamxett two of the finest anchorages in the world. These made Malta a strategically vital point for several centuries. This map illustrates how Ottoman Imperial communications could be interrupted by the Knights of St John based at Malta. It was in an effort to rid themselves of this menace and also to acquire the strategically vital archipelago that the Great Siege of 1565 was conducted.

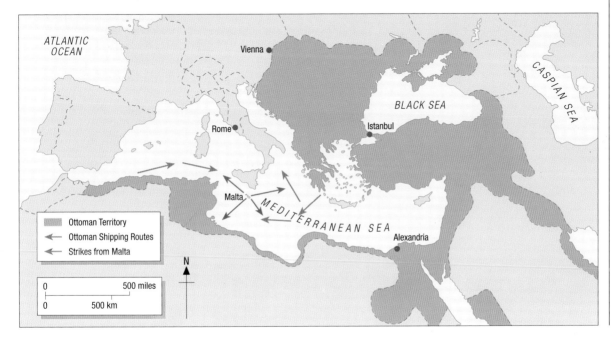

ATLANTIC OCEAN

Vienna

CASPIAN SEA

BLACK SEA

Rome

Istanbul

Malta

MEDITERRANEAN SEA

Alexandria

Ottoman Territory
Ottoman Shipping Routes
Strikes from Malta

N

0   500 miles
0   500 km

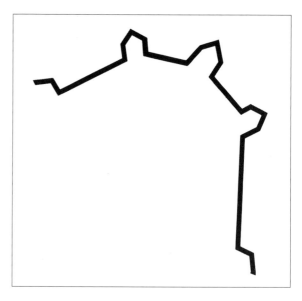

ABOVE Before gunpowder artillery – tall, thin, ramparts with towers. (Author's collection)

RIGHT Post gunpowder artillery – low thick ramparts, bastioned for enfilade fire. (Author's collection)

The Hospitaller Knights of the Order of St John of Jerusalem arrived in Malta in 1530, 'when the Emperor Charles V, enfeoffed them with the island of Malta, together with Tripolis, and the islands of Gozzo and Comino, under the condition that they should wage an incessant war against the pirates and infidels', as Sir Bernard Burke put it in 1858. Between their arrival and the Great Siege of 1565, they constructed or improved the three principal harbour fortifications of St Elmo, St Michael and St Angelo, and fortified the bases of the Birgu and Senglea peninsulas. Edward Gibbon describes them thus:

> the firmest bulwark of Jerusalem was founded on the knights of the Hospital of St. John, and of the temple of Solomon; on the strange association of a monastic and military life, which fanaticism might suggest, but which policy must approve. The flower of the nobility of Europe aspired to wear the cross ... The austerity of the convent soon evaporated in the exercise of arms: the world was scandalised by the pride, avarice, and corruption of these Christian soldiers ... But in their most dissolute period the knights of the hospital and the temple maintained their fearless and fanatic character: they neglected to live, but they were prepared to die, in the service of Christ; and the spirit of chivalry ... has been transplanted by this institution from the holy sepulchre to the isle of Malta.

In the current context it is enough to know that Gibbon's description, though he appears to have conflated the Hospitaller and Templar orders, requires little in the way of augmentation, except to point out two further particular skills that the Knights had acquired by the time of their arrival in Malta: those of fortification and seamanship. The first can be ascertained by perusing the defences constructed by them on the island of Rhodes and elsewhere in the Dodecanese, but principally the city of Rhodes itself, whilst evidence for the second can be found in accounts of their activities as 'Christian corsairs'. Their stay on the island of Rhodes had lasted a little over two centuries until they had been defeated at the second siege in 1522. Charles V of Spain made the grant of Malta as a new home for the Order, though it came together with the fortress of Tripolis (Tripoli) on the North African mainland. This isolated outpost was forced to capitulate to the Ottomans in 1551, but the retention of Malta by the Knights meant that communications with it, and other Ottoman interests in North Africa, were constantly threatened by the 'organised piracy' by which they lived.

The Knights under siege

The 16th-century Ottoman State was cast in an imperial and expansionist mode and one of its principal historians, Halil Inalcik, has argued that between 1526 and 1596 there was no question of international politics with which it was not involved. In other words it was a world power at a period when those territories that bound the Mediterranean formed a significant portion of the world. During the early period of the rule of Sultan Süleyman I, who ruled from 1520 to 1566 and whose appellations included 'the Magnificent' and 'the Lawgiver', great advances in Ottoman power were made. These included the conquest of Rhodes, the capture of Buda in 1529 (though the same year also saw defeat at Vienna) and the annexation of Hungary in 1541. These successes, however, were the high points of Ottoman expansion and despite the conquest of Cyprus in 1570/71 – the last great military success – the years 1565 and 1566 marked the beginning of a halt in Ottoman advances and the start of a decline, albeit a very slow one, in the fortunes of the empire.

The year 1565 was of course when Süleyman's command that 'this nest of vipers' that Malta had become under the Knights be 'smoked out' was put into practice. History records that the resultant Great Siege was unsuccessful, despite the apparent weakness of the Knights' position. They were greatly outnumbered and only had three sets of poorly sited and constructed fortifications in the harbour area, the main focus of the Ottoman attack. However, fortifications are force multipliers – they allow smaller numbers to defy greater numbers with a superior prospect of success than if fighting on open ground. Sieges have almost always been costly in every sense of the word. According to 'the oldest military treatise in the world', written around two millennia before 1565, the 'worst policy of all is to besiege walled cities'. The skilful leader, Sun Tzu the author of this treatise tells us, captures his enemy's cities without laying siege to them. Unfortunately for practical exponents of the art of war, he is silent on how this may be achieved, merely noting that it should be. The Knights were unable to construct more than three sets of fortifications in the vital harbour area, but they were determined that 'skill' alone would not suffice the Ottoman army that attacked them in 1565 – they would have to 'lay siege' in order to capture them. (A detailed account of the Great Siege can be found in Campaign 50: *Malta 1565* by Tim Pickles, published by Osprey.)

It has been stated by several authors that the Knights in 1530 were not at first enamoured of their new home as it compared poorly to Rhodes. Whatever the truth of this, the fact is that having survived the Ottoman siege despite the eventual fall of St Elmo, they undertook a hugely expensive and concerted effort to make the harbour area as impregnable as possible; having fought valiantly for their territory they now desired to keep it at all costs.

Survival

Malta was not some uninhabited wilderness in 1530 and the arrival of the Knights, according to the Maltese historian Sir Themistocles Zammit, writing in 1926, was not universally welcomed by the indigenous population. However, there appears to have been little attempt, at least initially, by the Knights to overly interfere with the existing social order; the seagoing propensities of the new overlords meant that their attention was mainly centred on the harbour area. Indeed, the commission that had surveyed the island as a possible home for the Knights had little good to say about it in general, with the exception of the harbour area:

> On the western coast, there are neither smaller nor larger bays, and the beach is extremely rocky. On the eastern coast, however, there are numerous promontories, smaller as well as larger bays and two particularly beautiful large harbours, sufficiently large to accommodate fleets of any size.

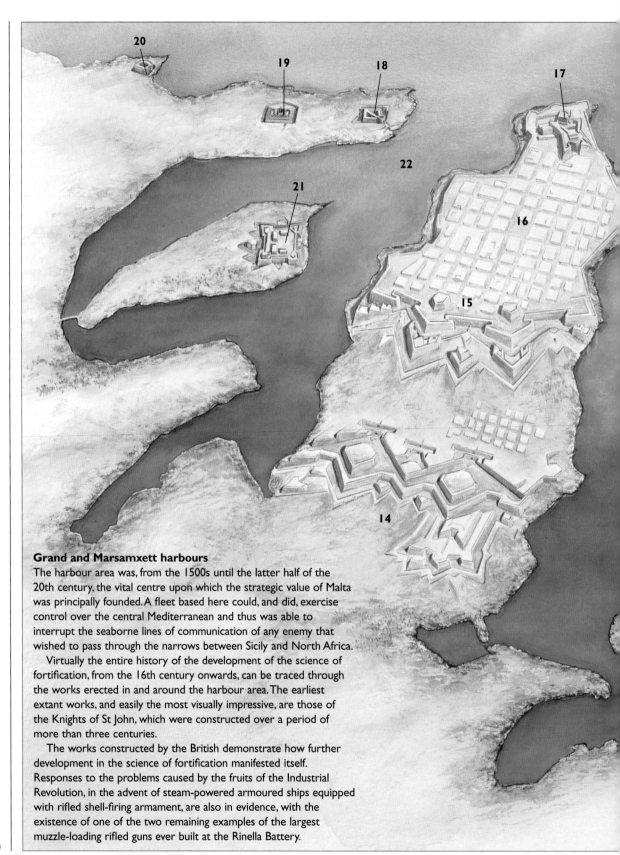

Grand and Marsamxett harbours

The harbour area was, from the 1500s until the latter half of the 20th century, the vital centre upon which the strategic value of Malta was principally founded. A fleet based here could, and did, exercise control over the central Mediterranean and thus was able to interrupt the seaborne lines of communication of any enemy that wished to pass through the narrows between Sicily and North Africa.

Virtually the entire history of the development of the science of fortification, from the 16th century onwards, can be traced through the works erected in and around the harbour area. The earliest extant works, and easily the most visually impressive, are those of the Knights of St John, which were constructed over a period of more than three centuries.

The works constructed by the British demonstrate how further development in the science of fortification manifested itself. Responses to the problems caused by the fruits of the Industrial Revolution, in the advent of steam-powered armoured ships equipped with rifled shell-firing armament, are also in evidence, with the existence of one of the two remaining examples of the largest muzzle-loading rifled guns ever built at the Rinella Battery.

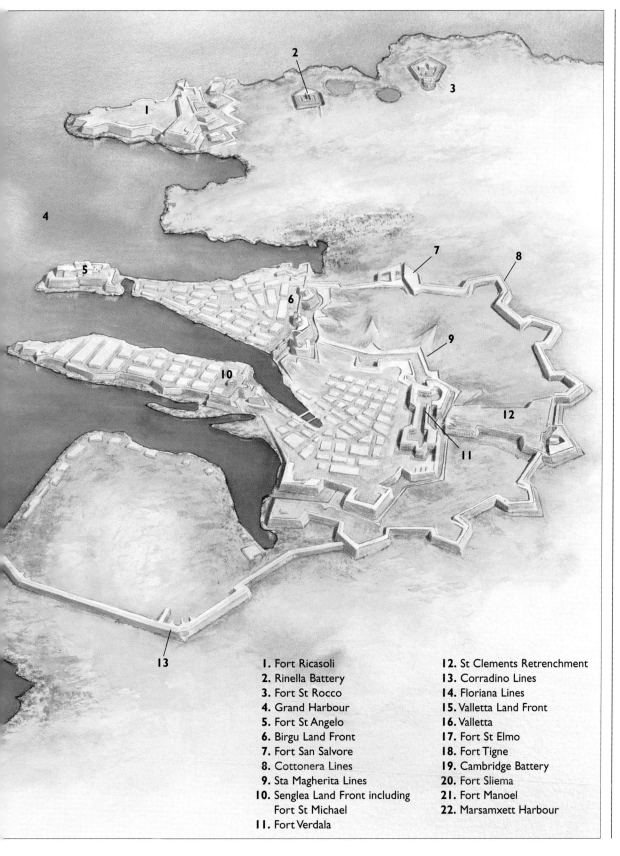

1. Fort Ricasoli
2. Rinella Battery
3. Fort St Rocco
4. Grand Harbour
5. Fort St Angelo
6. Birgu Land Front
7. Fort San Salvore
8. Cottonera Lines
9. Sta Magherita Lines
10. Senglea Land Front including Fort St Michael
11. Fort Verdala

12. St Clements Retrenchment
13. Corradino Lines
14. Floriana Lines
15. Valletta Land Front
16. Valletta
17. Fort St Elmo
18. Fort Tigne
19. Cambridge Battery
20. Fort Sliema
21. Fort Manoel
22. Marsamxett Harbour

Conversely the Maltese nobility centred their attention on the inland city of Mdina, the capital of the island. Mdina was one of the three fortified places on the archipelago, the other two being the Citadel at Victoria on Gozo and the Sea Castle (*castrum maris*) in the Grand Harbour on the tip of the Birgu peninsula. The defences of these places were considered totally inadequate against contemporary artillery, yet progress in renovating or reconstructing them was slow, probably due to a lack of resources combined with a reluctance to fully consider Malta as the order's permanent home. However, as the Knights had decided to base themselves around the Grand Harbour it followed that they had to strengthen their position there. Accordingly, the medieval sea castle was reinforced and upgraded, becoming Fort St Angelo and the village on the landward side enclosed by a wall, though this work took nearly ten years to complete. The Mdina defences were also modernised, though the work took even longer and was not totally completed until after the Great Siege. These two fortified places successfully resisted an Ottoman raid of 1551, when Ottoman ships sailed into Marsamxett and disembarked their troops. Finding the resistance too strong, they re-embarked and headed for Gozo, where the Citadel was taken, as was the outpost at Tripoli. Tripoli was irrecoverable, but the Citadel was repaired after the raiders had departed, though it was not modernised.

This raid, which was on a large scale with the raiders arriving on a fleet of around 100 ships, emphasised the fragility of the Knight's hold on Malta and the magnitude of the Ottoman threat. In terms of numbers alone this was formidable. Immediately prior to the Great Siege the Knights managed to muster a force estimated at a maximum of less than 10,000 men, whilst the Ottoman attackers are estimated to have landed somewhere between two and a half and four times that number from a fleet of some 200 ships. In order to protect themselves against the vastly greater numbers that could be deployed against them more fortifications were hastily begun and completed within a year or so under the supervision of a commission of three knights assisted by the military engineer Pietro Pardo. These consisted of Fort St Elmo, constructed on the tip of the Sciberras peninsula in order to deny access to Marsamxett harbour, and Fort St Michael at the base of the Isola peninsula in Grand Harbour. This latter position was reinforced in 1553 with a further wall, within which was to grow the town of Senglea, named after Grand Master Claude de La Sengle, though it was not fully completed by 1565.

The underlying principles of fortification are in themselves simple. However, like a great many other things they can be exceedingly difficult to achieve in practice; Fort St Elmo, for example, was built on ground that was overlooked and thus it could be, and was, dominated by enemy artillery. The fortified areas of Birgu and Senglea were also overlooked by the heights of San Salvatore and Sta Magherita. St Elmo only fell after a month of sustained effort and then after it had been virtually demolished by the Ottoman artillery firing from three different directions. This prolonged defence, an unexpected outcome of the mistaken Ottoman strategy of concentrating all resources on it in an effort to gain Marsamxett harbour, was amongst the chief factors in the failure of the Great Siege of 1565. However, following the Ottoman departure there was no guarantee that subsequent greater attempts would not be undertaken.

BELOW TOP A smooth-bored muzzle-loading iron cannon mounted on a wooden carriage to fire through an embrasure. This particular example of the type of ordnance used by the Knights of St John is mounted on St Michael's bastion at the Citadel, Gozo. (Courtesy of P. Evans)

BELOW BOTTOM A view from St John's demi-bastion of the curtain wall and *orillon* of St Michael's bastion, the Citadel. (Courtesy of P. Evans)

New construction, reconstruction, and the decline of the Ottoman threat

The history of the period following the victory in the Great Siege up until the year 1792 records a more or less constant programme of fortification undertaken by the Knights, with a particular concentration on properly securing the strategic epicentre around the harbours. The dangers that an unfortified Sciberras peninsula posed to the control of the harbours, and to the fortifications and fortified areas in Grand Harbour, had been pointed out prior to 1565, though circumstances had prevented any measures being taken to overcome these dangers. Despite the apparent urgency of the matter, the final decision to construct what was to become the city of Valletta was not taken until March 1566, but, once it had been made, construction proceeded with some speed, financed and supported by several Catholic European monarchs and Pope Pius IV. Indeed, it was the Pope who provided the services of one of his best military engineers, Francesco Laparelli, to design the new fortress. Laparelli arrived in Malta at the end of December 1565 and stayed some four years before handing over the work to Gerolamo Cassar. In 1571 the Order transferred its convent from Birgu to the new city, the construction of which extended the land front on the Sciberras peninsula some one kilometre inland and covered the highest parts. The buildings inside these fortifications were constructed on military lines and built to a grid pattern that allowed the utilisation of spaces between them and the fortress walls for the assembly of troops.

The year 1571 also saw Ottoman power diminished somewhat by their defeat at the naval battle of Lepanto. This battle was fought between a combined Christian fleet consisting of Spanish, Venetian and Papal ships, augmented by the galleys of the Knights of St John, who had a large part in the victory according to some commentators. Commanded by John of Austria the fleet of the 'Holy League' numbered about 200 galleys, whilst the Ottoman fleet under Uluç Ali Pasha had some 208; they were thus evenly matched in terms of numbers. Despite this the battle ended with the virtual destruction of the Ottoman navy, a mere 40 galleys escaping destruction or capture. According to accounts of the conflict, approximately 15,000 Turks were slain or captured, some 10,000 Christian galley slaves were liberated and much booty was taken.

The victors, however, lost over 7,000 men. Among the allied wounded was Miguel de Cervantes, who lost the use of his left arm, but fortunately survived to write *Don Quixote de la Mancha*. Lepanto was the first major maritime Ottoman defeat by the Christian powers and it ended the myth of Ottoman naval invincibility. The battle was decisive in the sense that an Ottoman victory would have made them supreme in the Mediterranean, whilst their defeat meant increasing difficulty in maintaining communications with territories in the west. This meant that naval forces in Tunis, Algiers and Tripoli no longer formed a regular part of the Ottoman fleet, but acted even more on their own initiative than before. However, even with these disadvantages Ottoman power remained formidable, and the potential threat to Malta still loomed large.

Accordingly, the completion of Valletta marked merely the starting point of a whole series of extensive fortifications, the object of which were to further secure the harbour area. That such precautions were necessary was a point reinforced in the year 1588 when the Spanish fleet, a major component of any counter to Ottoman naval dominance in the Mediterranean, was destroyed in its attempt to attack England. The loss of the Spanish Armada tilted, at least potentially, the balance of naval superiority back towards the Ottoman Empire.

The low battery attached to the flank of the Citadel on Gozo. Note the greater thickness of the ramparts facing the front of the work. (Courtesy of P. Evans)

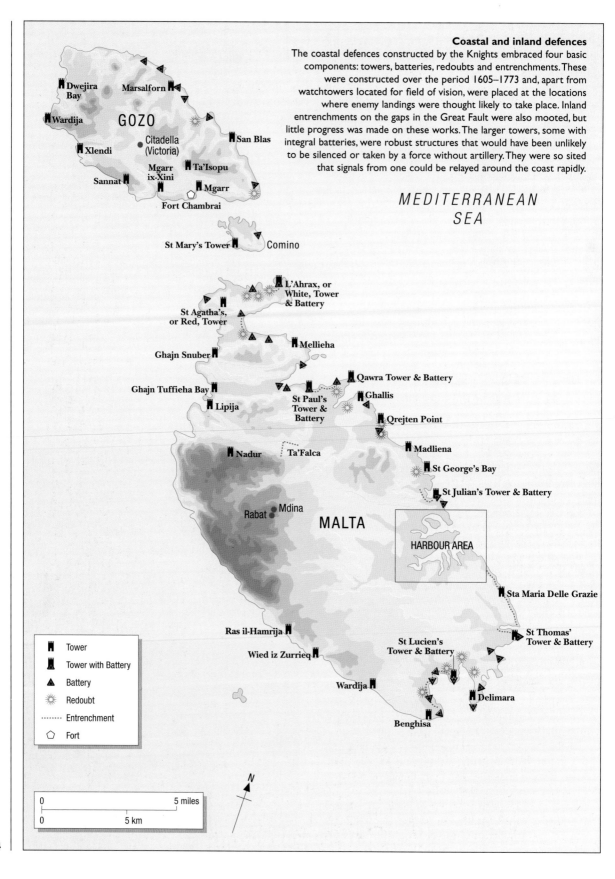

Coastal and inland defences

The coastal defences constructed by the Knights embraced four basic components: towers, batteries, redoubts and entrenchments. These were constructed over the period 1605–1773 and, apart from watchtowers located for field of vision, were placed at the locations where enemy landings were thought likely to take place. Inland entrenchments on the gaps in the Great Fault were also mooted, but little progress was made on these works. The larger towers, some with integral batteries, were robust structures that would have been unlikely to be silenced or taken by a force without artillery. They were so sited that signals from one could be relayed around the coast rapidly.

MEDITERRANEAN SEA

GOZO

Dwejira Bay
Marsalforn
Wardija
Citadella (Victoria)
Xlendi
San Blas
Mgarr ix-Xini
Ta'Isopu
Sannat
Mgarr
Fort Chambrai

St Mary's Tower — Comino

L'Ahrax, or White, Tower & Battery
St Agatha's, or Red, Tower
Mellieha
Ghajn Snuber
Ghajn Tuffieha Bay
Lipija
St Paul's Tower & Battery
Qawra Tower & Battery
Ghallis
Qrejten Point
Nadur
Ta'Falca
Madliena
St George's Bay
St Julian's Tower & Battery
Rabat ● Mdina
MALTA
HARBOUR AREA
Sta Maria Delle Grazie
St Thomas' Tower & Battery
Ras il-Hamrija
St Lucien's Tower & Battery
Wied iz Zurrieq
Wardija
Delimara
Benghisa

Legend:
- Tower
- Tower with Battery
- Battery
- Redoubt
- Entrenchment
- Fort

0 — 5 miles
0 — 5 km

N

Fort St Elmo

This plate depicts Fort St Elmo as it appeared in the last decade of the 17th century following the construction of the Carafa bastions along the shoreline. The original fort on the site was constructed by the Knights of St John in the 1550s, being completed in 1556, and was the focus for the Ottoman attacks during the Great Siege of 1565. Reconstruction of the fort along more substantial lines followed the lifting of the siege, but it was rendered more or less immune to land attack by the construction of the fortified city of Valletta to its front. The rear of the fort was secured in 1687–89 by the construction of the bastioned fortifications.

Entrenchment and overstretch

Fort St Elmo was strengthened with the addition of a bastioned sea-facing wall and Valletta itself was augmented with further landward-facing works. These were designed to keep enemy artillery as far as possible from the main defences. An extensive series of new fortifications designed by the Italian engineer Pietro Paolo Floriani was begun in 1635. The Floriana Lines, as they came to be called, were an ambitious project, arguably too ambitious, and they were criticised on the grounds of expense and the size of the garrison that would be required to effectively man them. Commitment to the works was accordingly sporadic, and was further lessened by the decision to begin another enormous system to protect the landward fronts of the Senglea and Birgu peninsulas.

Known as the Sta Magherita Lines, these defences were designed by Vincenzo Maculano da Firenzuola to secure the heights that allowed an invader to oversee, and thus fire into, the two areas, both of which had been renamed after the siege; Birgu becoming *Città Vittoriosa*, whilst Senglea was re-christened as *Città Invicta*.

The level of financial investment required to simultaneously undertake these two projects strained the resources of the Knights too far and work soon halted until such time as further money could be raised – a cycle that repeated itself. The resultant stop–go nature of the construction meant that it was only during the 18th century that the works were completed, a condition exacerbated as far as the Sta Magherita Lines were concerned by an even more ambitious plan to fully enclose them within another even more extensive line of fortifications: the Cottonera Lines. Designed by the Italian engineer Antonio Maurizio Valperga and named after Grand Master Nicholas Cotoner, who had them commissioned in 1670, these have been accurately described as the 'most ambitious work of fortification ever undertaken by the Knights of St John in Malta'. A simplified version of this series of works was only completed in the 1760s.

In the year 1670 Valperga was also responsible for designing another important fort in the Grand Harbour, Fort Ricasoli, named after the knight Giovanni Francesco Ricasoli, who financed a large part of the project. This fort was constructed to secure an obvious weak point in the harbour defences – the promontory known as Gallows Point where Ottoman artillery had been based in 1565. The construction of this fort commenced in June 1670 but it was only in 1698 that it was finally fitted with its complement of artillery.

It was a quarter of a century later before another potentially weak point in the defences of the harbour area was addressed. Though dominated by the northern side of the Valletta fortifications, the small island known as the *Isoletto,* situated within Marsamxett harbour, was only fortified for the first time in 1723 with the construction of Fort Manoel. Designed by Charles François de Mondion, the Knights' contemporary resident engineer, it was named after the Grand Master who financed the work.

A bronze barrel dating from the 17th century mounted on a British 19th-century 14lb iron carriage. (Courtesy of P. Evans)

It is somewhat surprising to note that Fort Manoel was the first construction designed specifically to protect Marsamxett harbour, though with the entrance guarded by the rebuilt Fort St Elmo and the southern shore covered by the Valletta defences perhaps the lack of such security was more apparent than real. In any event, the last harbour fort to be constructed was also designed to protect Marsamxett harbour and was built on Dragut's Point, where Ottoman artillery had been placed to subdue St Elmo in 1565. Fort Tigne was begun in 1792 and when completed in 1794 was a very small work by contemporary standards. However, its design by another of the Knight's engineers, Stefano de Tousard, has been authoritatively described as 'probably the most revolutionary and influential of all the fortifications built by the Knights'.

The outer ring

The first priority of the Knights was to secure the harbour area against attack and for the greater portion of the 16th century they directed most of their resources and efforts to achieving this. The relocation of their convent from Birgu to Valletta in 1571 was a symbol of their confidence in the newly fortified city, though the continuing Ottoman threat necessitated the construction of further defences over the following centuries.

However, during the early years of the 17th century the Knights directed their attention away from the harbour area and began to address the problem of coastal fortification over the rest of the island. As it was an island the only way to attack Malta was to launch a seaborne operation against it – amphibious warfare. It is axiomatic amongst practitioners of such warfare that the most hazardous operations are those that involve making an opposed landing against a defended point on a coast. For example, in the 1982 operation against the Argentinean-occupied Falkland Islands, the commander of the British amphibious force categorised his requirements for landing areas as: 'good … exits … out of direct enemy gunfire range and not … prone to immediate counter attack.'

To thus provide the maximum amount of hazard for any invader, and the greatest degree of protection for the defenders, coastal fortifications were constructed. Throughout the period there were two main types of threats to the Maltese coastline. The first was an invasion proper, as per the Ottoman attack of 1565, and the second consisted of raids by smaller numbers of troops. Any return of an Ottoman invasion force would only have been effectively countered by withdrawal into the fortifications around the harbour area; the coastal defences could not have been expected to resist such a force. Smaller-scale raids by corsairs, however, were a different matter.

Corsairs were pirates who operated in the Mediterranean between the 15th and 18th centuries and many works refer to there being two kinds of corsairs: Muslim and Christian. The Muslim corsairs had bases along the Barbary Coast of North Africa, principally the ports of Algiers, Tunis and Tripoli. The latter was captured in 1551 by one of the most notable of the corsairs, Dragut, who owed allegiance to Süleyman I. Indeed the Sultan had conferred upon him the titles of Imperial Governor of Tripoli and Admiral of the Grande Porte, and entrusted him with something approaching commander-in-chief status during the Great Siege, where he was killed. Dragut had raided Malta on several occasions between 1540 and 1565, carrying off virtually the entire population of Gozo into slavery in 1551. The point being that although many of the corsair raids were little more than of nuisance value they could cause great devastation, and, although the connection between these pirates and the Ottomans was somewhat disrupted after the battle of Lepanto in 1571, these may well have been spoiling attacks or reconnaissance missions.

The need to deter and defeat corsair raids then became a matter of importance, and in order to achieve this no fewer than 31 towers were constructed in three distinct phases. Five towers were erected: at St Paul's Bay (1609), Marsaxlokk (1610), St Thomas Bay (1614), Sta Maria delle Grazie (1620) and, somewhat later, at Mellieha (1649). Two were also constructed on Gozo, at Mgarr (1605) and Marsalforn (1616), and one on the small island of Comino (1618).

Between 1636 and 1657 six smaller watchtowers were constructed at Ghajn, Tuffieha, Lippija, Qawra Point, St George's Bay and Wied iz-Zurrieq. Three towers

ABOVE TOP Constructed in 1618 the tower on the south-west cliff-top of Comino dominates the channels between Gozo and Malta. St Mary's tower is still used by the Maltese Defence Forces. (Courtesy of P. Evans)

ABOVE BOTTOM The armament of the coastal towers was generally light, and this photograph shows a 6lb cannon of the type used during the rule of the Knights. St Paul's Island is in the background. (Courtesy of P. Evans)

were also constructed on Gozo at San Blas, Xlendi and Dwerja. These were augmented by a further 13 towers erected in the two year period of 1658–59: at Delimara, Wardija, Hamrija, St Julian's, Qalet, Marku, Ghallis, Madliena, Benghisa, L'Ahrax, Triq il-Wiesga, Xrop l-Ghagin and Ghajn Hadad. Two further towers were constructed on Gozo in the 1660s, Mgarr-ix-Xini (1661) and ta' Isopu near Nadur (1667). The final tower constructed by the Knights was at Marsalforn, again on Gozo, built in 1760, but the near century-long time lapse between this last construction and its nearest predecessor was not an indication of satisfaction with the existing defences, but rather what might be termed a 'swing of the pendulum' in the eternal debate about whether any invading force should be opposed on the beaches, or allowed to land and then faced.

The network of additional gun batteries and other defences, construction of which began in the early 1700s, is evidence of a swing back to the 'fight them on the beaches' philosophy. This followed on from a report, presented in 1715, pointing out that there were several bays, in an arc encompassing the whole southern, eastern and northern coastlines, where an invader could shelter a substantial fleet and disembark troops: Marsaxlokk Bay (where the invaders of 1565 had landed), Marsaskala Bay, St Thomas Bay, St Julian's Bay, Madliena, St Paul's Bay and Mellieha Bay, not to mention the northern coast facing the island of Comino. Between 1715, when construction commenced at Marsaxlokk, and 1792, the date of completion of the final work on Gozo, 34 coastal gun batteries were built. Designed to engage enemy vessels that approached the shore, these batteries were complemented by some 20 infantry redoubts, whose function was to provide a strongpoint for infantry, though some were also armed with artillery to prevent any invaders from gaining a viable beachhead.

Schemes for entrenchments also figured in the coast defence report adopted in 1715. These were designed to reinforce weak areas that had already been identified. Rather than fieldworks made up of trenches (Malta is rocky and has very little naturally occurring surface soil of sufficient depth) these were to take the form of infantry lines – vertical walls constructed so as to be somewhat similar in plan to the larger versions found around the harbour area. It appears, however, that only on Gozo was the work of constructing these entrenchments actually commenced as it was calculated that the manpower demands involved in using them in anger were so great as to make them unviable. The Knights were probably not the first, and certainly not the last, to discover that guarding a long coastline in such a manner is so costly in terms of consumption of resources and manpower as to be almost impossible. Accordingly, it was decided to shorten the line of defence, and the place chosen for constructing this new line was along a ridge, known as the Great Fault, which more or less bisects Malta in an east–west direction, separating a region characterised somewhat by ridges and valleys to the north from more rolling countryside to the south.

Running from Fomm ir-Rhi Bay on the west coast to Bahar ic-Caghaq on the east, the Great Fault forms a natural barrier of high ground and is thus difficult to approach undetected. It does, however, have several weak points from the military engineering point of view in that there are several gaps and gently sloping portions that would present little in the way of a natural obstacle to any attacker. Chief amongst these are the gaps at Naxxar, Falca and Bingemma, and the eastern coastal area near Madliena. The decision to fortify these areas was taken in 1722, as well as to construct an entrenchment near Mdina.

However, whilst the northern part of Malta saw its defence line shortened, the same was not to apply to the more sensitive southern portion. The decision to construct entrenchments along the line of the coast from this area, from Ricasoli southward to Marsaxlokk, and northward from Dragut Point to St Julian's Bay, was taken in 1723. Following this, plans for an even more ambitious scheme were drawn up, which visualised some 30 further batteries being constructed on the various headlands around the coast, and, rather fantastically, the erection of a more or less continuous wall around the entire coastline of both Malta and Gozo.

St Paul's Bay Tower

The St Paul's Bay Tower is the oldest surviving coastal tower in the Maltese archipelago. The tower was strongly constructed and armed with two 6-pounder cannon mounted on the roof. It was garrisoned by a small force of perhaps six men, whose living quarters were on the first floor. This upper room was accessed via the exterior staircase and then across a drawbridge. Access to the ground-floor storeroom was through a hatch in the floor. There are two turrets on the southern side of the roof for landward defence and a smaller structure on the north-west corner for a sentry to watch the sea. Mounted below this is an opening very like a machicolation, which was a projecting gallery through which missiles or other substances could be dropped on those below. Networks of additional towers were constructed between St Paul's Bay and Valletta, as well as more outlying areas, so that any incursions could be reported quickly by visual means.

Situated on the tip of the Senglea peninsula in Grand Harbour, this vedette, or sentry post, is one of the most famous sights in Malta due to its decoration. (Courtesy of P. Evans)

The physical remnants of this policy can be seen in the entrenchments constructed on the Qawra peninsula, at Armier Bay, Mellieha, Spinola, St Julian's, Birzebugga, Marsaskala and along the coast from Ricasoli to Zonqor Point. The first three locations are above the line formed by the Great Fault, and the decision to construct them is surely evidence of a certain indecisiveness with regards to the decision of 1722, whilst the Ricasoli–Zonqor works are in line with the policy decision of 1723. By 1763 nearly a kilometre of entrenchments had been constructed, with a further kilometre in place in the Marsaxlokk Bay area. However, work on these defences ceased in 1773 and many of the extant works were allowed to fall into disrepair. This was also the state of the entrenchments along the Great Fault, though occasional attempts at restoration were made. These efforts mark the last of the Knight's works on the fortification of the Maltese archipelago other than the completion of Fort Tigne in 1794.

The Ottomans never seriously attempted to attack Malta again after their repulse in 1565, though their potential to do so was the motivational factor behind the fortification after that event and there were many scares and alarms. The only other landing in any force after the Great Siege was a major raid in 1614. Some 5,000 men in 60 vessels landed at St Thomas's Bay, but were successfully repulsed with little damage. There were various other minor incursions by corsair vessels, but these were piratical rather than military operations, though of course this may not have been obvious at the time. There were many instances, however, in 1635, 1640, 1645, 1714, 1722, 1731/32, and 1760/61, when serious attacks were feared and expected, though these never materialised.

Perhaps the worst scare since the Ottoman capture of Cyprus in 1571 came in 1669/70 when an Ottoman resurgence appeared to be looming following their occupation of Candia, now Crete. The Venetian Republic had occupied this island since the 13th century, and it had been the object of serious Ottoman attentions for over two decades prior to the eventual conquest in 1669. The Turks renamed the city of Candia (Iraklion), after which the island was named, 'Megalokastro' (big castle) due to the immensity of the fortifications they inherited there. Dating from 1462, though the construction period spanned a century, a massive wall, over 60m thick in places and with a perimeter of around 4.5km, was built. Designed by the Venetian military engineer Michele Sammicheli, the defences incorporated 12 bastions.

The end result then of over two centuries of expected Ottoman invasion saw the Maltese archipelago fortified to an extent probably unprecedented in any similar-sized area. These were strong defences as relevant at the end of the 18th century as they had been in the 16th.

Design and development of the Hospitaller fortifications

In 1938 Mao Zedong wrote that 'to the present day, all weapons are still an extension of the spear and shield', and the advent of gunpowder artillery may be represented as one of those occasions when the balance of effectiveness between these two elements swung in favour of the spear. This swing was not quite the revolution that Gibbon's picturesque prose suggested when he wrote that 'the proportion of the attack and defence was suspended, [when] this thundering artillery was pointed against the walls and towers which had been erected only to resist the less potent engines of antiquity'. That this is so can be adduced by considering the fact that artillery was in use for some time before it began to have any effect on the design of fortification; the earliest cannon threw so very light a projectile that they had insignificant effect on masonry. However, in the middle of the 15th century the art of cannon founding was much developed in France and iron cannon balls were introduced together with greatly strengthened guns. Charles VIII unveiled his new artillery system to the rest of Europe with his invasion of Italy in 1494. His rapid successes in taking castles and fortified towns demonstrated the obsolescence of the old defences and it became necessary to create a new system. The lead came from Italy, where the mental Renaissance combined with constant physical conflicts served to stimulate the greatest intellects. Famous names such as Leonardo da Vinci, Michelangelo and Machiavelli applied their minds to the problems raised by the improvement in cannon. Not for nothing were the first renowned military engineers of the gunpowder age of Italian origin and it was their influence that dictated the design of the Maltese fortifications.

Fortification has a double tactical object, which Sir George Sydenham Clarke summarised thus in 1890:

> The only scientific Fortification is that which enables the defender to use his weapons to the best advantage, while minimizing the potency of the weapons of the attacker.

Achieving these aims requires two elements from the fortifications: protection for the defenders and obstruction of the attackers. These principles are enduring though the means by which they may be achieved vary greatly according to time and place and are subject to evolution and occasional revolution. The advent of efficient artillery meant that the destruction of the defences, as well as the suppression of defensive fire, could be accomplished at a greater distance than was previously possible. The other side of this coin though was that the power of the defence could also be projected further. Thus the fortifications constructed by the Knights encompassed elements of protection and obstacle; the protection shielded the defender from the attackers weapons, whilst the obstacle prevented the attacker from coming to close quarters and delayed him under fire. These elements were constructed in accordance with the latest contemporary European thinking, where the science, or art, of fortification had been pondered and distilled.

Protection was of two basic sorts: direct and indirect. Direct protection was given by a structure strong enough to stop or deflect missiles hurled at it, but the value of this was reduced somewhat if the defender had to expose himself to return the enemy's fire, or to otherwise resist his attempts to destroy the defences. Indirect protection was given by distance and concealment and European engineers had solved the problem of protecting the wall from breaching by artillery by the expedient of sinking it in a ditch.

Generally speaking, therefore, the ditch became a characteristic feature of the works of fortification constructed on Malta, serving the double purpose of supplying material for a rampart and allowing the wall to be sunk for concealment, as well as providing an obstacle. When the wall or escarp was lowered, the obstacle offered by the ditch was increased by revetting

BELOW TOP During the Great Siege, de Valette ordered the drawbridge of Fort St Angelo destroyed in order to discourage any thought of retreat. This view shows the water-filled ditch that protected the landward side of the fort. The bridge nearest the camera is modern. (Courtesy of P. Evans)

BELOW BOTTOM St John's Bastion is the central of the three bastions, the left and right being St James' and St Michael's respectively, on the Valletta land front. A counterguard further protected the ditch, now obscured with foliage, and situated behind the bastion was St John's *cavalier*. (Courtesy of P. Evans)

Fort Tigne

Constructed on Dragut Point, named after the Ottoman corsair who had caused batteries to be mounted there during the Great Siege, Fort Tigne was the last fortification constructed by the Knights, and their first to depart from the bastioned trace, being akin to the polygonal in its system of defence.

Diamond-shaped in plan with a substantial circular tower at the rear, a ditch equipped with three large counterscarp galleries surrounded it. From these galleries, which were reached via tunnels from within the work, radiated a series of pre-bored countermines. There was a large fortified barracks running from the tower to the furthest angle and the whole work was considered to be capable of 'considerable resistance' according to the opinion of British officers who examined it in 1800.

When originally armed the work contained some 28 cannon of various sizes and six mortars, and the British used the site for coastal defence purposes up to and including World War II. Today, the only obvious remnant of the work is the circular tower.

the far side of it with another wall, or counterscarp, and, beyond this, some of the material excavated from the ditch was formed into the glacis; that is, piled up to increase the protection given to the escarp wall and sloped gently in such a manner as to be swept by fire from the ramparts. The introduction of the counterscarp wall though, if unmodified, would have prevented sorties from the ditch against the besiegers, an essential part of an 'active' defence. To overcome this, a space was left at ground level behind the glacis that allowed room for troops to assemble. This space became known as the covered way, sometimes rendered as covertway, and with this development the elements of the profile of Malta's fortifications were more or less complete.

The bastioned trace

All the Knights' major works, except the last, utilised the bastioned trace, a technique of fortification that dominated the science of European fortification for 300 years. Bastions project the defence forward beyond a simple linear wall, and thus allow defenders to subject an attacker to fire from more than one direction. In the bastioned trace there is no 'dead' ground, and the idea, with other refinements such as, for example, the erection of *cavaliers* behind the parapet of the curtain or in the bastions, held the field until near the end of the 18th century. The Italian engineers, who were considered the leaders throughout most of the 16th century, started it; the French, who took the lead, though always in competition with the Dutch, in the following century, developed it, as well as a large proportion of the vocabulary of fortification that has come down to us.

When viewing the plans or traces of Hospitaller fortifications, it is well to keep in mind the fundamental considerations that dictated their design, which was the need to prevent attackers from getting over the top or breaching the defences. Mining was of course a different and distinct problem but not an easy option on Malta. Generally speaking, in the days of pre-industrial warfare there was only one method of getting attacking troops into a fortress; they had to run or creep towards the defences and then physically occupy them. If the defences were undamaged this might be achieved by climbing over them, a process known as escalade; or, if a portion of them had been destroyed or pulled down, by storming through the resultant breach. All the fortification systems that were constructed by the Knights, no matter how apparently complex, had as their object the obstruction or prevention of this operation by bringing effective fire onto those preparing for and attempting the attack.

In order to overcome a bastioned work the attackers first had to approach it over the glacis under forward fire from the defences, including perhaps fire from detached *lunettes* on the crest of the glacis. They then had to cross the main obstacle, the ditch, by descending the counterscarp and ascending the scarp. The

Taken from Marsamxett harbour, pictured, from the left, are St Andrew's Bastion, St Michael's Bastion, St Michael's Counterguard and St John's *Cavalier*. Something of the sheer scale of these works can be grasped in this picture. (Courtesy of P. Evans)

scarp might be protected by a *tennaile*, a wall constructed in front of the scarp to protect it. Bastions and outerworks projecting into, or constructed in, the ditch would subject those in the ditch to crossfire. This could be from several directions dependent on circumstances. Because bastions were designed to be within range of each other, an attempt to attack one would mean crossfire from others. Areas requiring greater protection would be equipped with outerworks, such as ravelins, *lunettes*, counterguards and bonnets constructed in the ditch. These projected firepower further forward and intensified the level of crossfire. An attacker that succeeded in taking an outerwork would then be subject to fire from the main defences, which would still have to be overcome. The various elements of the bastioned trace were then mutually supporting and offered defence in depth plus intensified enfilading fire. They thus epitomised the principles of fortification in providing the maximum amount of hazard for the attacker, with the greatest degree of protection for the defenders, and were a product of what might be termed the 'gunpowder age'.

All the Hospitaller Maltese fortifications were constructed during this age prior to which, as is shown by the works on Rhodes, the trace of their fortifications was comparatively simple. It was, basically, a wall provided with towers at suitable intervals. The foot of the wall could be seen and defended from above and for this purpose projections, or machicoulis galleries, were constructed on top with openings through which missiles or other material could be dropped or poured. Towers also afforded refuges for the garrison in case of a successful escalade and from them the top of the wall could be attacked from a flanking position and thus be exposed to crossfire, or enfiladed as the technical term has it. This form of fortification, a tall, relatively thin, towered wall, had survived basically unchanged for many centuries and the three fortified sites that the Knights inherited in 1530 were all of this type, which the adoption of effective gunpowder-fired weapons rendered obsolete.

The Knights, as has been pointed out, were skilled in the science of fortification prior to their arrival in Malta and, in addition, could afford the services of several French and Italian military engineers. Unsurprisingly then the fortifications constructed under their auspices reflected the latest thinking over the periods of time they were constructed.

The commission of Knights who visited the Maltese islands in 1524 with a view to appraising their suitability as a home for the Order were not geologically expert, as their words made clear: 'The island of Malta is nothing but a rock of soft sandstone called tuff.' In fact, the stratigraphic succession of Malta, from top to bottom consists of: Quaternary sediments, Upper Coralline limestone, greensand, blue clay, Globigerina limestone (named for the fossilised microscopic protozoan creature found within it), and Lower Coralline limestone. One of the characteristics of the Globigerina limestone is that it is easily sawn into uniform blocks and hardens when exposed to the air. This ensured that the majority of the Knights' fortifications were constructed of it up until the beginning of the 18th century. It was discovered, however, that this stone deteriorates when exposed to high humidity, and so from the late 17th century coastal fortifications were constructed from the Lower Coralline limestone, which suffers less from this defect.

The Knights themselves did not labour, nor did their retinue, so the manual work of constructing the fortifications was undertaken by more common folk. In fact slaves would have

One of the smaller types erected between 1636 and 1657, the tower at Qawra Point is now incorporated into a pool/bar complex. This view shows the tower as close to its original configuration as it is possible to get. The final courses of masonry forming the roof are modern. (Courtesy of P. Evans)

formed a large proportion of the workforce and the Maltese population, though they would have to be remunerated, were also employed on the works. One source speaks of 8,000 workmen toiling on the fortification of what would become Valletta in 1566, though does not mention from whence they came and this figure is believed to have been much exaggerated. Certainly, whilst there would have been a requirement for a large number of artisans to complete the skilled portion of the work, the 'donkey work' would have needed thousands.

The construction of fortified areas has a dual purpose: that of providing defensive protection, and to form a secure base from which offensive operations may be carried out. The institutionalised exploitation of slavery not only provided a vital component in the Knights' defensive schemes, but also played as important a part in their offensive arm. This is so because slaves provided the power for the offensive arm of their war-machine: the galley. Slave-powered galleys were rendered anachronistic by the advent of improved sailing vessels and it may be argued that with the Ottoman threat to the Christian world greatly abated during the 1680s and 1690s, when the encroachment of Ottoman military power was halted in Europe, the Knights and the culture they represented was similarly so. As J. F. C. Fuller put it: for nearly 250 years, from 1483 to 1683, the one topic of European politics was 'the Turk'. After the latter date that topic changed. With the diminution of the Ottoman threat the Knights' *raison d'être*, to wage 'incessant war against the pirates and infidels', had also gone and this was underlined when other Mediterranean states built up substantial naval forces to defend their coastlines during the 17th and 18th centuries. Ironically, perhaps, it was one of these fleets, though under a rather different command than envisaged, that eventually provided the means for turning the Knights out of their island fiefdom.

The fall of the Knights

The 1789 French Revolution was a disaster for the Order of St John. The Knights were unable to prevent the Revolutionary Government in France from seizing the Order's properties there and depriving many of them of their incomes. Thus impoverished and having, over a period of time, forfeited the goodwill of the Maltese population, the demise of the Order was perhaps inevitable.

Napoleon Bonaparte was only 29 years old when he persuaded the Revolutionary Directorate that the wisest strategy in pursuing war with Britain involved attacking Egypt rather than invading the British Isles. Accordingly, a large expeditionary force was assembled at Toulon consisting of 13 French and two Venetian ships-of-the-line; 14 frigates and some 400 transports capable of carrying some 36,000 troops. This fleet left port in May 1798 and by 9 June had reached the waters around the Maltese archipelago, by which time it had been reinforced to a strength approaching 500 vessels.

Napoleon Bonaparte is remembered by history as one of that select group who possessed, in Clausewitz's phrase, 'the genius for war'. Given the density and quality of the fortifications he was facing in attempting an amphibious operation against Malta, it might have been thought he would certainly need to deploy that genius in order to succeed. He did not need to do so because the organisation that had spent over two and a half centuries, and unimaginable quantities of treasure, in making their island home as impregnable as was humanly possible had succeeded. The system of fortifications constructed at such cost had turned the whole of Malta into as unassailable a fortress as was possible. But, whereas in 1565 the fortifications crumbled under enemy fire but the morale of the defenders remained solid, this time the reverse was the case, exacerbated by a 'fifth-columnist' element amongst many of the Knights themselves.

The French made multiple landings on the morning of 10 June, including one on the strategically insignificant island of Gozo, with about half their force, some 15,000 troops. These landings occurred at places previously foreseen as likely

The French invasion of 1798. The French made multiple landings, including one on the strategically insignificant island of Gozo, with about half their force, some 15,000 troops. These landings occurred at places previously foreseen as likely invasion points, and which were thus heavily fortified against such an eventuality. Napoleon had neutralised the potency of these defences by subversion, and by landing virtually unopposed gained a significant advantage at minimal cost. This advantage was translated into victory the next day when the Knights surrendered, and on 12 June Napoleon landed and installed himself in the Parisio Palace on Merchants' Street. From here he set about conferring the benefits established by the French Revolution upon the people of Malta.

invasion points and which were thus heavily fortified against such an eventuality. Napoleon, however, had neutralised the potency of these defences by subversion, and by landing virtually unopposed gained a significant advantage at minimal cost.

By the end of that day the majority of the island had been occupied. Negotiations began on the morning of 11 June and that same evening a peace was signed and the island handed over. The following day Napoleon himself landed and installed himself in the Parisio Palace on Merchants' Street. From here he supervised the drawing up of a treaty between the Order and the French, under the terms of which the Knights were granted pensions for their lifetimes in return for leaving the islands. They left. Napoleon stayed only a short while before resuming his journey to Egypt, but before he left he set about ensuring that the benefits established by the French Revolution would be conferred upon the people of Malta. This, however, was a gift that they did not necessarily appreciate.

In fact, the process whereby the Maltese population had become alienated from their former rulers was replicated, though in drastically truncated form, in the case of the military regime installed by the French forces. The causes of this estrangement seem to have mainly revolved around Republican anti-clerical policies, which did not sit well with a culturally homogenous population that was overwhelmingly observant in composition. Whatever the cause, within three months of the regime change there was an armed uprising by the indigenous population.

The French garrison was not strong, consisting of a little over 3,000 infantry and five companies of artillery. They were well armed and disciplined and took the only course of action reasonably open to them – they manned the harbour fortifications, thus violating the Napoleonic maxim that 'an army that stays within its fortifications is beaten'. This action left the countryside to the Maltese, who raised a military force numbering around 10,000, of whom only about one-quarter were adequately armed. They were also able to deploy a number of artillery pieces taken from the coastal batteries, towers and entrenchments. The Maltese leaders were not experienced in the military art and, though they displayed a high degree of resourcefulness, were inexpert in the art of siege warfare. Their situation was exacerbated by a scarcity of provisions, and by internal division, but even so this force took up positions

RIGHT Constructed in 1647/48 there are several unusual features, which appear to be decorative rather than functional, relating to this tower, most notably the colour, the result of paint rather than an attribute of the building material. Unsurprisingly, known as the 'Red Tower' it has decorative splayed merlons crowning the four roof turrets and a surrounding 'star-trace' low wall. (Courtesy of P. Evans)

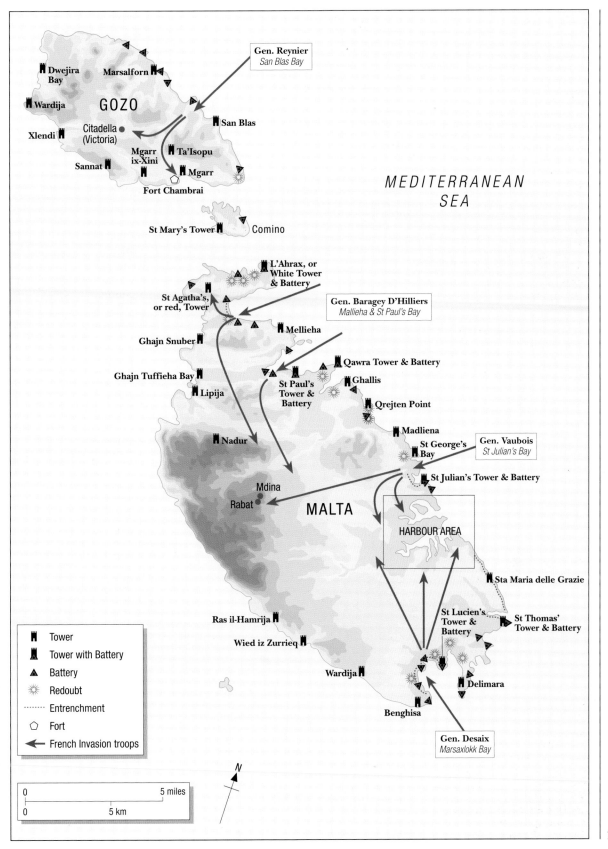

Gen. Reynier
San Blas Bay

Dwejira Bay

Marsalforn

GOZO

Wardija

Xlendi

Citadella (Victoria)

San Blas

Mgarr ix-Xini

Ta'Isopu

Sannat

Mgarr

Fort Chambrai

MEDITERRANEAN SEA

St Mary's Tower

Comino

L'Ahrax, or White Tower & Battery

St Agatha's, or red, Tower

Gen. Baragey D'Hilliers
Mallieha & St Paul's Bay

Ghajn Snuber

Mellieha

Ghajn Tuffieha Bay

Qawra Tower & Battery

Lipija

St Paul's Tower & Battery

Ghallis

Qrejten Point

Nadur

Madliena

St George's Bay

Gen. Vaubois
St Julian's Bay

St Julian's Tower & Battery

Mdina

Rabat

MALTA

HARBOUR AREA

Sta Maria delle Grazie

Ras il-Hamrija

St Lucien's Tower & Battery

St Thomas' Tower & Battery

Wied iz Zurrieq

Wardija

Delimara

Benghisa

Gen. Desaix
Marsaxlokk Bay

Tower
Tower with Battery
Battery
Redoubt
Entrenchment
Fort
French Invasion troops

0   5 miles
0   5 km

N

The trace of the wall surrounding the tower can be clearly seen in this aerial photograph. It is thought that the purpose of this wall was to make the tower appear large and formidable. However, since it contains a chapel dedicated to St Agatha it seems equally as likely that the embellishments were decorative. (Courtesy of P. Evans)

around the harbour defences and constructed extempore fortifications around them – lines of contravallation. These were constructed more to keep the French from breaking out than as a position from which to conduct siege operations.

Since neither force was strong enough to defeat the other, the situation developed into a stalemate that could only have been broken by outside intervention. One attempted relief by a French force was thwarted by British sea power, but in no way could the Royal Navy be said to have total command of the sea, and the arrival of another relieving force could not be discounted. Accordingly the French garrison was not in an absolutely hopeless situation and thus adopted the strategy of 'sitting it out' in order to gain time. They were estimated to have enough food for 18 months.

The Maltese were in no such position and required foreign assistance if they were to prevail. This eventually came, in September 1798, in the form of a small squadron of vessels under the command of Captain Alexander Ball. Ball set up a blockade of the harbour area and landed some 500 British and Portuguese marines, though this supplement to the Maltese forces was completely insufficient to stage anything like an effective attack on the French-manned fortifications. It was not until something over a year later, in December 1799, that a greater measure of reinforcement was undertaken, but then only a brigade-strength force, which was not itself significantly enhanced until July 1800 when another 1,500 men were deployed on the island.

Even with this increase there were never enough troops or logistical support to seriously contemplate an assault on the French, who remained virtually immune from attack behind the massive fortifications. However, since they were effectively isolated from relief by the success of the naval blockade, 'one of the finest exhibitions of "Admiralty" in the whole war' according to Fred T. Jane, it became a matter of time and on 4 September 1800, with both food and hope of relief exhausted, they came to terms with the British. This arrangement was undertaken over the heads of the Maltese forces, who, despite their contribution to the situation, were excluded from the surrender negotiations mainly because the French refused to negotiate with them and the British, anxious not to delay proceedings, did not contend the matter.

There is evidence that this sidelining of the Maltese fighters did not take place within the context of British self-interest, inasmuch as, at that time, Britain had no wish to maintain control of the islands, merely to deny them to an enemy. However, having denied Malta to the current enemy it was the realisation that future denial to future enemies might best be accomplished by being in occupation that heralded a change of policy from one of temporary to permanent occupancy. In 1815 Malta was proclaimed a Crown Colony.

British Imperial Malta – 1800–1939

By this time Britain had become a naval superpower and Malta, both inordinately well defended and situated in a strategically significant position, assumed a position of considerable importance. The Royal Navy provided the British with the offensive component that the Knights had lacked and a substantial fleet based in Grand Harbour could enforce Britain's will and protect the Mediterranean passage to India. This route, even prior to the advent of the Suez Canal exponentially increasing its importance, was a vital Imperial artery, which Napoleon's Egyptian campaign of 1798 had been intended to sever. However, it was the case that during this period there was very little in the way of what would today be called a 'National Security' policy and the War Office and the Admiralty tended to develop plans and even operations in isolation. (This, incidentally, was a practice that continued into the 20th century, as can be seen by the somewhat disorganised meeting of the Committee of Imperial Defence in 1911, when the Army and Navy presented plans for a forthcoming war that bore no relation to each other.)

Unsurprisingly, upon taking possession of the islands one of the first tasks undertaken by the new overlords was a survey of the fortifications they had inherited. This was no academic exercise, as Revolutionary France remained a significant naval threat and still laid claim to the territory. The immediate concern therefore was to establish a defensive plan in the event of an enemy landing, which it was thought would probably occur at the same sites that had been used in 1797. Accordingly, the existing defences at St Paul's Bay and Marsaxlokk were manned using both Maltese troops, the former militia of the Knights, and British regulars.

Aside from the actual fortifications themselves, the British also came into possession of a significant amount of ordnance. Exactly how much is difficult to calculate, but when the French were under siege in the harbour area they had available to them 598 cannon, 49 mortars and 10 howitzers. In addition to this the fortifications outside the harbour area, including Gozo and Comino, were armed with some 300 cannon. It seems then that the British, in taking possession of the islands, also took possession of not far off 1,000 artillery pieces of varying size. However, keeping such a variety of artillery operational created major logistical problems, in that each calibre required shot to suit. There was also the problem of mixing up

BELOW LEFT Constructed in 1878, Fort Mosta exemplifies the polygonal system of fortification, with the keep being protected by a ditch. Also featured are casemates. Not visible are three counterscarp galleries armed with carronades designed to sweep the ditch clear of any intruders. Its final armament, mounted on 'disappearing' carriages, consisted of two 152mm guns. (Photo by Joe Sammut from *The Victoria Lines*, Malta, 1996)

BELOW RIGHT Projecting from the scarp of a polygonal fort, a *caponier* allowed flanking fire along the ditch. This is a demi-*caponier* because only one side has been loopholed, for musketry in this case. (Courtesy of P. Evans)

ABOVE LEFT Sunk into a drop-ditch (a ditch within the main ditch but at 90 degrees to it) this view through a *caponier* loophole shows the virtual impossibility of attackers being able to survive in, or get across, the main ditch. Because of the drop-ditch, the exposed portion of the *caponier* presented only a small target. (Courtesy of P. Evans)

ABOVE RIGHT Fulfilling a similar function to a *caponier*, this gallery built into the angle of the counterscarp covered the length of the ditch. The last smoothbore muzzle-loading ordnance in use in the British Army, the carronade, was employed in counterscarp galleries until the beginning of the 20th century. (Courtesy of P. Evans)

the ammunition for the various pieces. One officer complained of this in 1852, stating that there were:

> piles of French shot on the Batteries by the side of English guns, just of a size to render the guns unserviceable if one of the shots were to be, by mistake, put into one of the English guns. I am informed that it is intended to remove all the French cannon and shot here, but year passes after year and this is not done.

Rationalisation might have been thought to be an urgent requirement therefore, but in fact it was not undertaken for some 60 years, until 1859/60. By this time many of the weapons and fortifications had become obsolete. There were many technological advances during the early to middle years of the 19th century that saw the gradual demise of the smoothbore gun, bastioned fortifications and wooden ships.

The relevance of the Knights' works until the middle portion of the 19th century ensured that no significant construction was undertaken by the British until after that time. This was compounded by the presence of the Royal Navy's Mediterranean fleet based at Grand Harbour, rendering incarnate the philosophy that the domination of the waters around an island was the best method of ensuring its security against invasion. Accordingly, the early British efforts were restricted to making minor improvements to the existing fortifications, though proposals for constructing additional works to protect perceived weak points in the harbour area were made.

One proposition for improving the existing works that was far from minor concerned the Cottonera Lines. Because these had never been completed as originally envisaged they somewhat resembled a reversion to the pre-gunpowder age in that they took the form of a lengthy wall, bastioned but without a ditch or outworks. One further factor militating against the effectiveness of the fortifications in the Cottonera/ Sta Magherita area was the large open space between the two lines. The existence of this area raised the possibility that an attacker, able to penetrate the unfinished Cottonera Lines, would be able to manoeuvre unmolested and isolate them from the Sta Magherita Lines. The British constructed a work in 1849 to divide the space between the lines into two and thus provide flanking fire against any enemy that ventured into the area. St Clement's Retrenchment was the result and it was able to command each half of the space between the lines.

The artillery pieces shown in this 1899 photograph of the Victoria Lines are 6in. BL howitzers on siege carriages. These short-barrelled weapons threw a heavy shell at a high angle, up to 35 degrees, for 'searching' concealed positions and dead ground. (Photo courtesy of Richard Ellis Ltd.)

Further work to strengthen the area was also undertaken in the creation of Fort Verdala from the central bastions of the Sta Magherita Lines; a conversion rather than new construction. Further internal strengthening of the harbour area defences took place in 1854 with the construction of a battery within Grand Harbour itself to provide support for the guns located in Fort St Angelo on the Birgu peninsula. Located on the southern side of Valletta this consisted of two tiers of casemates and was christened the Lascaris Battery after a former Grand Master of the Knights in whose garden it was sited.

Outside the harbour area there were extensive coastal defences and these were kept in commission until further study in the 1820s held them to be too weak, particularly with regard to the towers. The

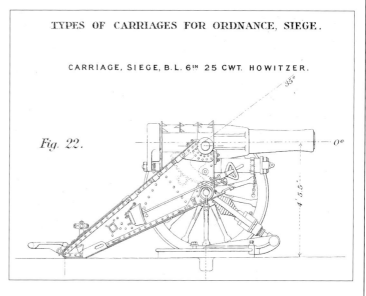

TYPES OF CARRIAGES FOR ORDNANCE, SIEGE.

CARRIAGE, SIEGE, B.L. 6^{IN} 25 CWT. HOWITZER.

Fig. 22.

A drawing of a 6in. BL howitzer on a siege carriage. Note the spring mounted between the platform and the carriage, and the hydraulic buffer beneath the barrel, to absorb the recoil. This carriage could be modified in the field, by removing the wheels and bolting on a 'top carriage', to fire at an angle of 70 degrees. (Phillips)

British form of coastal defence was the Martello Tower, many of which were constructed in the British Isles, which were robust structures compared to their Knightly equivalent. Indeed, in 1830 it was proposed that many of the Knights' towers be demolished so that they could not, in the event of an invasion, 'afford cover and protection, facilitating the further debarkation of troops'. In 1832 this point was reiterated, along with a description of their condition: 'The towers and redoubts are … much out of repair and in [a] dilapidated … condition.' Fortunately for posterity the proposal was never put into practice and 16 of them maintained their role. The rest were decommissioned and handed over for civil use.

The demise of Napoleonic France at Waterloo in 1815 proved but a respite in the challenge to the ascendancy of the Royal Navy. Denied a chance of quantitative equality by the superior capacity of the British, France, in its various post-Napoleonic incarnations, made moves to establish a qualitative lead by introducing shell-firing guns in 1837. This had profound implications for ship design; the detonation of a shell in a wooden structure caused a primary fire at the site of the explosion and numerous secondary conflagrations where the red-hot splinters landed. Thus shellfire was fatal to wooden ships, the types on which the Royal Navy's supremacy was founded. If Britain's entire naval inventory was not rendered obsolete at a stroke, it was only because there was no

The 100-ton RML, one of 12 such weapons built by Armstrong of Newcastle upon Tyne, was the largest muzzle-loading weapon ever constructed. The *Regia Marina* used eight of these and, as a counter, the British sited two of the remaining four at Malta in the Cambridge and Rinella Batteries. They were capable of hurling a 907kg shell some 6,400m. (Courtesy of P. Evans)

alternative to wood at that time. Armouring vessels with iron could provide a greater degree of protection against shellfire, which was rendered longer ranging and more accurate with the introduction of rifled muzzle-loading (RML) cannon in 1842.

The French were again qualitatively in advance of the British in constructing such a vessel, when in 1858 they launched the first ironclad warship, the frigate *La Gloire*. This was, literally, a ship clad in iron with 125mm of iron plate over a wooden hull. She was powered by steam, though also fully rigged. Armed with 16 160mm muzzle-loading rifled shell-guns *La Gloire* represented a fundamental change in naval architecture and fighting power. Naturally, the British responded and comprehensively trumped the French in 1859 by beginning the construction of a vessel that was not just a wooden ship plated with iron, but one that was designed and built almost entirely of that material. HMS *Warrior*, which resembled a 'snake amongst rabbits' in Palmerston's phrase when he saw it amongst conventional vessels, was the first of a type that was to evolve to a culmination only in the 20th century, but the point is this: fortifications constructed out of masonry now became vulnerable to armoured ships firing explosive shells. The far more destructive effects of tapered explosive shells replaced the battering effect of solid round shot, which the maritime fortifications around the harbour area had been designed to withstand. Lord Nelson had once cautioned of the danger inherent in 'laying wood before walls'; laying iron before walls was a somewhat different matter, especially if those walls were no longer proof from naval gunfire delivered at previously unheard of ranges.

The British entrench

In 1860 a Royal Commission, convened to report on the state of British defences at home, came to the conclusion that the reliance that the country had formerly placed in the Royal Navy for protection against invasion had been outstripped by the new technologies carried to sea in steam-powered warships. In a complete about turn it recommended that fortifications be constructed at strategically important installations such as the Royal Dockyards, Woolwich, Portsmouth, Portland, Dover and Cork. This departure had been mooted previously and sparked a furious controversy. One venerated admiral with much experience in amphibious warfare had put it thus as far back as 1845:

> Protective harbours … may be likened to nets, wherein fishes seeking to escape, find themselves inextricably entangled … [n]o effective protection could be afforded in such ports against a superior naval force equipped for purposes of destruction … [t]he hasty adoption of such measures, and the voting of the vast sums required to carry them into execution, are evils seriously to be deprecated. It is therefore greatly to be desired that those in power should pause before proceeding further in such a course.

The top-carriage of the 100-ton gun, showing the nine rollers per side (only two now survive) that allowed it to retract up the 4-degree angle of the traversing carriage after firing. It was necessary for it to be fully retracted before reloading could take place via one of the reloading turrets situated on either side. There were two of these in order that one would always be ready for action. (Courtesy of P. Evans)

This photograph shows the traversing carriage and one of the reloading turrets. The circular plates at the rear cover the two cylinders that absorbed the recoil and returned the gun to its firing position. In order to be loaded, the weapon had to be fully retracted and then traversed fully to either side and aligned with the port in the relevant reloading turret. A hydraulic rammer then inserted a charge and shell, and the weapon was then elevated, the top-carriage returned to the front of the traversing carriage and traversed to engage its target. The cycle could be completed in six minutes. (Courtesy of P. Evans)

Armed with the recommendations of a Royal Commission, the project went ahead and the subsequent fortifications, or 'Palmerston's Follies' as they became known, formed the largest programme of fortification ever undertaken in Britain, with some 76 works of various sizes eventually constructed. What happened in Britain also took place on Malta, and some ten years later the island was similarly outfitted, though on a reduced scale.

The coastal defences at the entrance to the harbour area, basically Fort St Elmo, Fort Tigne and Fort Ricasoli, were to be re-armed with modern artillery for repelling maritime attacks by armoured ships, as these works were considered too weak to withstand attack by explosive shell. Accordingly, these 'Keys to Malta' were accorded the greatest priority, though between 1872 and 1878 other coastal forts were also constructed. These were: Fort Sliema (1872), St Rocco (1873), St Lucian (1874), Pembroke (1875), St Leonardo (1875) Delimara (1876) and Tas-Silg (1879).

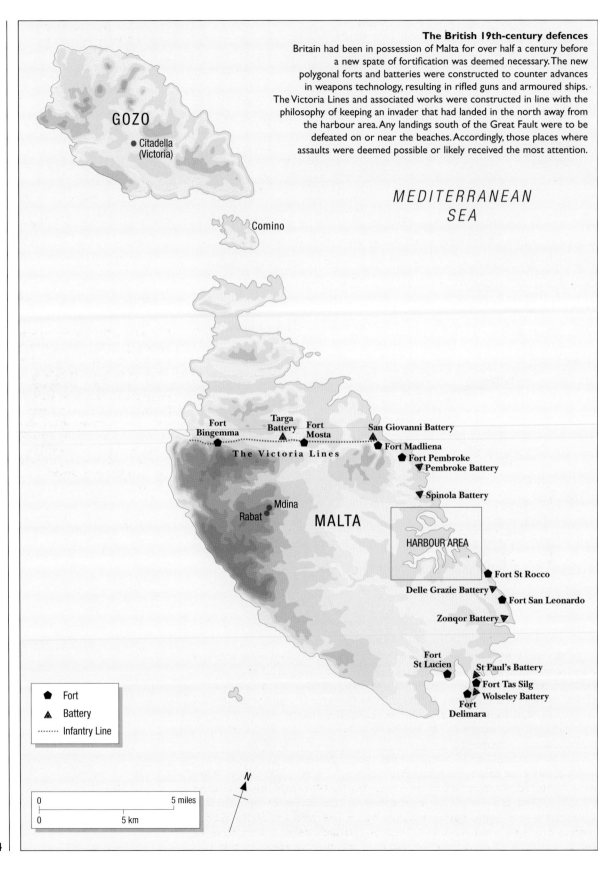

The British 19th-century defences

Britain had been in possession of Malta for over half a century before a new spate of fortification was deemed necessary. The new polygonal forts and batteries were constructed to counter advances in weapons technology, resulting in rifled guns and armoured ships. The Victoria Lines and associated works were constructed in line with the philosophy of keeping an invader that had landed in the north away from the harbour area. Any landings south of the Great Fault were to be defeated on or near the beaches. Accordingly, those places where assaults were deemed possible or likely received the most attention.

GOZO

Citadella (Victoria)

Comino

MEDITERRANEAN SEA

Fort Bingemma

Targa Battery

Fort Mosta

San Giovanni Battery

Fort Madliena

Fort Pembroke

Pembroke Battery

The Victoria Lines

Spinola Battery

Rabat Mdina

MALTA

HARBOUR AREA

Fort St Rocco

Delle Grazie Battery

Fort San Leonardo

Zonqor Battery

Fort St Lucien

St Paul's Battery

Fort Tas Silg

Wolseley Battery

Fort Delimara

Fort
Battery
Infantry Line

N

0   5 miles
0   5 km

The 17th-century Madliena Tower juxtaposed with a 19th-century 280mm RML. (Photo by Joe Sammut from *The Victoria Lines*)

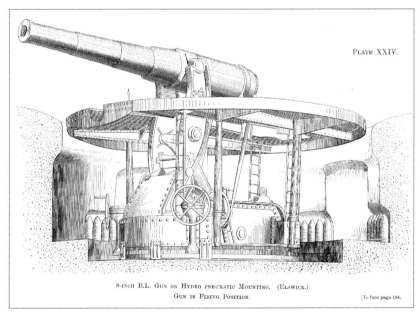

PLATE XXIV.

8-INCH B.L. GUN ON HYDRO PNEUMATIC MOUNTING. (ELSWICK.)
GUN IN FIRING POSITION.

[To face page 194.

Known as the Elswick mounting, from Armstrong's Tyneside factory where they were constructed, these devices used the energy developed in the recoil of the gun to return it from its firing position to its loading position. During this transition, the movement of the weapon was used to compress air by way of a piston. This pneumatic energy was then itself used to raise the weapon back up to its firing point via a hydraulic ram. (Sydenham Clarke)

At the same time a series of works designated as coast-defence batteries were constructed. Rather than being mere emplacements for artillery, several of these, in terms of scale, protection and offensive armament, were practically indistinguishable from works designated as forts. The Cambridge (1878) and Rinella (1879) Batteries were also built during this period to house 'replies' to innovative ships commissioned into the navy of a relatively recent arrival on the international scene – Italy.

The National Italian Navy was created on 17 November 1860, when the regional navies of Sardinia, the Bourbons, Sicily, Tuscany and the Papal States were combined. Four months later, on 17 March 1861, it became the *Regia Marina Italiana* following the proclamation of the Kingdom of Italy. The traditions of the various navies stretched back many years and in the current context it is sufficient to mention the strong Italian presence at the battle of Lepanto in 1571. However, the reputation of this fleet suffered a tremendous

Put into use between 1880 and 1890 disappearing gun mountings were developed for weapons of 6in. and more. However, they were not generally considered successful because of their great complexity and expense, combined with a very slow rate of fire. They were thus replaced by *barbette* carriages in which the gun and mounting were in a pit protected by a concrete parapet with only the gun muzzle and shield visible. This increase in visibility was more than compensated for by greater increases in efficiency. (Sydenham Clarke)

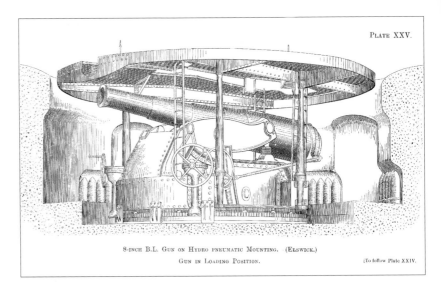

PLATE XXV.

8-INCH B.L. GUN ON HYDRO PNEUMATIC MOUNTING. (ELSWICK.)
GUN IN LOADING POSITION.

[To follow Plate XXIV.

setback at the battle of Lissa on 20 July 1866, when it fought against and was defeated by a smaller Austrian fleet.

Perhaps unsurprisingly, one of the first moves after Lissa was to reduce the Navy's budget, ushering in what the historian Aldo Fraccaroli called 'dark, sad years for the Navy, [as it was] relegated to a position of minor importance'. However, a revival began in the early 1870s, with the result that, according to Fraccaroli, 'the Italian fleet reached third place amongst the navies of the world in less than 20 years'. The first examples of the new fleet were the turret ships *Duilio* and *Dandolo*, both laid down in 1873, and, when completed, armed with the largest guns then in existence – four 450mm RMLs. Faster (15 knots plus) than any other battleships at the time of launching, in 1882 they were commented upon flatteringly by a then little known naval officer, Captain 'Jacky' Fisher, who was himself commanding the British response to them, the largest ship in the Royal Navy, HMS *Inflexible*, launched in 1876.

These two vessels, the first battleships in the world rigged only with a military mast and the first Italian two-shaft capital ships, were heavily armoured with a 546mm belt of Creusot steel, and 432mm of nickel steel turret armour; the turrets being mounted *en echelon* close together amidships. The guns, each weighing 100 tons were actually British built by Armstrong, and could each fire one 864kg projectile every 15 minutes, with a muzzle velocity of somewhere between 429 and 509m/s (1490–1670f/s). Given the proximity of Italian territory to Malta, it was feared that in the event of hostilities breaking out between Britain and Italy, these two vessels would be able to stand off Valletta and reduce the works around the harbour area to rubble with relative impunity. Accordingly, the decision was taken to mount identical weapons, originally four, but in the event only two, in batteries to the north and south of the harbour area. Hence the construction of Cambridge and Rinella Batteries, which mounted one of these monster weapons apiece.

The construction of these defences was a reflection of one event that transformed Malta from an important to a vital strategic British possession, the opening of the Suez Canal in 1869. This meant that the island now sat athwart a shipping route of crucial importance to the British Empire. The canal, built by a French company, profoundly altered the situation in the Middle East and more particularly the key British concern of access to India. Prior to its opening the sea route to India had involved travelling around the Cape of Good Hope. The quicker route through the Mediterranean had traditionally involved disembarking on the Syrian coast and travelling overland through Mesopotamia to the Persian Gulf. This was a journey entirely through Ottoman territory and

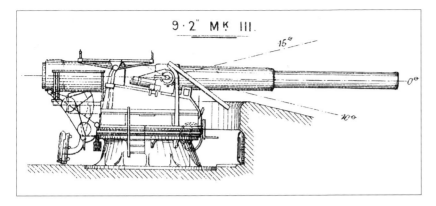

9·2" Mᴷ III.

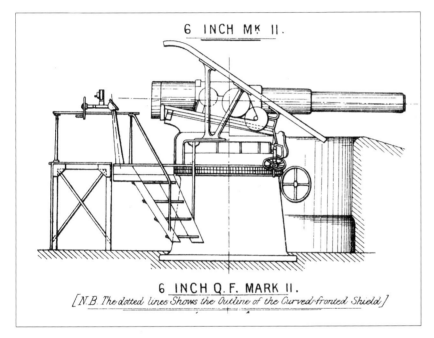

6 INCH Mᴷ II.

6 INCH Q.F. MARK II.
[N.B. The dotted lines Shows the Outline of the Curved-fronted Shield]

was thus dependent on Ottoman goodwill and stability, neither of which was considered reliable. Journeying through the canal, though it still involved passing through what was nominally Ottoman territory, greatly lessened this dependence, as Egypt was virtually independent and open to manipulation. As the sea route became the vital artery of empire, the secure possession of Malta became a vital British national interest and strengthening the defences assumed a higher priority than previously. This led to the reinstating of a scheme first initiated by the Knights, the fortification of the Great Fault.

Work began in 1875 on what were to be called the Victoria Lines in commemoration of the Diamond Jubilee of Queen Victoria in 1897. The first work constructed was a fort at Bingemma to protect one end of the line of the Fault, whilst Fort Madalena, started in 1878, fulfilled the same function at the other. A fort at Mosta, begun in 1880, covered the central position. The fortification of the Great Fault was completed by the addition of a fairly simple wall some 1.5m in height, reinforced at intervals with gun batteries and emplacements between the forts. This linear defence crossed several of the valleys that feature in the Great Fault by the expedient of constructing it upon bridges spanning these gaps. Further augmentation of the position as a whole was undertaken with the construction of Fort Pembroke, built to defend the coast in the gap between the eastern end of the Victoria Lines and Valletta.

Rinella Battery

Each built to house a single specimen of the ultimate expression of the RML weapon, the 450mm 100-ton gun, the Rinella and Cambridge Batteries were more or less identical.

The gun was *barbette* mounted on a carriage that itself weighed some 45 tons, with the whole being trained by hydraulic machinery. In order to load the weapon, the barrel was first run to the back of the carriage and then the whole mounting traversed 90°, right or left, and fully depressed. This operation brought the muzzle in line with one of the loading ports of the armoured loading chambers, and the gun was moved to the front of the carriage, when its muzzle would push open a shutter and protrude into the port. A hydraulic rammer pushed the 250kg charge and 907kg shell into the barrel. It could then be withdrawn back up its carriage, elevated to the required angle, traversed to face the target, and moved to the front of the carriage again ready for firing.

The battery was pentagonal in plan and the defensive system consisted of a ditch containing three *caponiers* with drop-ditches and a counterscarp gallery.

Incredibly the gun remains in position today, unlike its counterpart in the Cambridge Battery, and is one of only two in existence, the other being at Gibraltar.

Design and development of the British fortifications – the polygonal trace

All the new forts, as opposed to improvements made to the Knights' forts, built by the British in Malta were variations on the polygonal theme, featured somewhat in the Knights' Fort Tigne, which further developed the concept of indirect protection by concealment. This was necessary because of the advent of rifled artillery, which gave projectiles a much greater range and penetrative power and forced the builders of land fortifications to sink them lower into the ground in order to present less of a target by blending in with the surrounding area.

The vastly increased range of rifled artillery over its smoothbore predecessor also forced the adoption of the detached fort system, which comprised an outer screen of individual mutually supporting fortifications designed with the object of keeping the artillery out of range of the place being defended. This was the rationale behind the concept of the Victoria Lines protecting the harbour area. These detached works were essentially defended gun batteries, whether conceived as coastal defences, with their guns placed inside heavy masonry casemates protected by armour plating, or as inland forts with their guns mounted *en barbette*. A perimeter ditch flanked by vertical scarps and counterscarps protected the forts, though this ditch was narrower compared to those previously used, so that oblique incoming fire would be less likely to destroy the scarp. The flank defences of the ditch, no longer provided by bastions, consisted of either *caponiers* or galleries built into the counterscarp.

The linear nature of the infantry line, almost a reversion to the pre-gunpowder days of fortification, is noteworthy in this photograph of the Victoria Lines taken in 1899. It is also worth noting that these soldiers, as part of the non-indigenous population, would have suffered from 'Malta Fever'. Its cause was long obscure but was eventually identified as a microorganism transmitted in Maltese goats' milk. A commission headed by Col. David Bruce went to Malta in 1904 and three years later produced a report conclusively identifying the source of the problem. Banishing the milk from the military and naval diet in 1906 put a stop to the occurrence of cases and a vaccine was developed. The disease was named brucellosis after its discoverer. (Photo courtesy of Richard Ellis Ltd.)

ABOVE TOP The essentials of this powerful work of the Victoria Lines, near to the site of an earlier work by the Knights, are clear in this photograph. Note the substantial ditch and the loopholed parapet, which would have presented a small target to attackers whilst allowing defenders a good field of fire. (PRO W078 5301)

ABOVE BOTTOM The form of the infantry line is very clear in this picture and looks anachronistic when compared to the field entrenchments that became so much a feature of early 20th-century warfare. This was realised at the time and the entire Victoria Lines were deemed vulnerable after being 'penetrated' in exercises in 1900, and were subsequently abandoned in 1907. (Photo courtesy of Richard Ellis Ltd.)

These were the defining elements of the polygonal trace, which was so called because of its appearance in plan view.

Four counterscarp galleries featured in the Corradino Lines, which were built to deny the Corradino Heights overlooking Grand Harbour from the west to a potential enemy. Commenced in 1871, this fortified line ran from the face of St Paul's Bastion on the Cottonera Lines to Ras Hanzir on the southern shore of Grand Harbour, forming a shallow V in plan view, with a ditch 10m deep and 8m wide. Facing the point of this V, or salient angle of the work, was the largest of four counterscarp galleries, featuring two storeys, with the lower one level with the bottom of the ditch. This was perforated with large embrasures for smoothbore breech-loading carronades (short-barrelled large-calibre cannon), whilst the upper floor was fitted with loopholes for musketry. However, both the Corradino and Victoria Lines were abandoned as obsolete, in the case of the latter within seven years of completion in the first decade of the 20th century, and a return to the concept of repelling any invasion force from the beaches was adopted, though little was done in terms of building new works beyond those constructed during the last 20 years of the 19th century.

Further batteries, though with lesser weapons, were constructed after the completion of the Cambridge and Rinella Batteries at St Thomas Bay (St Paul's

GHARGUR RAVINE

Battery; 1881) and Marsaskala (Zonqor Battery; 1882). These works represent the last constructed to be armed with RML weapons, for technological change, and the latter portion of the 19th century was a time of rapid change, intervened to make them obsolete and see their replacement with breech-loading (BL) weapons.

The introduction of breech-loading artillery was itself complemented by another development in defensive power, the adoption of concrete. This material, later to be reinforced with iron and steel, quickly replaced masonry for new construction, and was used to augment existing works, so that by the last decade of the 19th century the artillery positions around the harbour area had been reinforced with concrete and reconfigured to take breech-loading artillery. This upgrading was itself complemented by six new works designed, between 1888 and 1910, to house mainly 9.2in. and 6in. BL guns, which were the types settled upon to form the staple armament of coast defences. These were the Delle Grazie Battery (1889), which departed from the norm in having two 254mm (10in.) guns, rather than 234mm (9.2in.) guns, Spinola Battery (1889), Garden Battery (1889), Wolseley Battery (1897), Pembroke Battery (1897) and Fort Benghisa (1910). The construction of Wolseley Battery heralded another change in the design of fortifications as it included provision for defensive machine-gun emplacements and barbed wire entanglements; devices popularly associated with World War I, which was to break out in 1914.

The demise of formal fortification

There were many lessons learned from World War I, amongst them that technology had once again, at least initially, swung the pendulum back in favour of the shield as against the spear, though only in the case of extempore fieldworks and not in the case of permanent fortification. This had been evident several decades previously with the introduction of the infantry rifle. In its muzzle-loaded version it had forced a revolution in tactics during the

'Wied' is a Maltese word equivalent to the Arab 'wadi' – dry riverbed. However, these can become flooded during periods of rainfall, hence the need to fortify them with bridge-like structures. Part of the Victoria Lines, this fortified bridge is constructed so that floodwater can pass under it. (PRO WO78 5301)

41

American Civil War. The defensive power of the single-shot breech-loader was exemplified during the Anglo–Zulu War of 1879, and in 1899 the British, to their consternation, discovered the phenomenon of the 'empty battlefield' during their conflict with the Boers, famously armed with Mauser magazine rifles, in South Africa. Sir George Sydenham Clarke, in the 2nd edition of his book on fortification, had said this in 1907:

> Among the developments of modern arms which in a special degree affect the defence, none is more potent than the magazine rifle … Now that the effective range of the Infantry weapon has been multiplied by more than twenty, and its rate of fire by at least fifteen, an immense power has been conferred upon the defence, which no Artillery progress has neutralized … There is no arm so potent in its influence on all questions of land defence as the magazine rifle.

Of course, following World War I the weapon that had impinged itself most on the popular consciousness was the machine gun, as its name suggests a device

This stop wall has openings to allow the draining away of rainwater from the slope behind it. (Photo by Joe Sammut from *The Victoria Lines*)

for discharging bullets at a rate which could render areas of ground impassable through the creation of a 'beaten zone'. Clarke had forecast this as well:

A view from the north-west of the Great Fault where it overlooks the coast at Bahar-ic-Caghaq. Fort Madliena was constructed there at the eastern extremity of the Victoria Lines. (PRO W078 5301)

> The fire of the Maxim gun, delivering about 700 bullets per minute, can be directed by one man ... In the special qualities of the machine gun there is a distinct advantage to the defence, arising from the fact that a few men occupying a small space can suddenly develop an intense fire over a particular area.

If fieldworks manned by troops with magazine rifles and machine guns, backed by copious quantities of artillery to their rear, had rendered the infantry attack a problematical exercise, then techniques of attack on permanent fortifications had rendered their future existence and validity equally doubtful. Put simply, all the techniques of fortification hitherto employed were recognised as redundant after 1918. Colonel Kelly stated it thus in his contribution to the 1929 Edition of the *Encyclopaedia Britannica*:

> The comparatively rapid and shattering fall of the Belgian fortresses in 1914 caused a complete revulsion against permanent fortification. Liège with its 12 armoured forts fell in 11 days after the opening attack, and eight days after the first use of the German 17in. howitzers ... Namur withstood only four days' bombardment and four of the main Antwerp forts were rendered untenable in three. On the eastern frontier of France the barrier fort of Manonvillers was reduced to ruins in two days.

Colonel Kelly envisaged the future of fortification as being restricted to:

> zones of defence, without large permanent works ... Within these zones the fortifications will not take the form of elaborate forts, but will consist of dispersed and concealed tank-proof localities, with the intervals between them well covered by obstacles and the fire of all arms.

Thanks mainly to the decision of Italy not to join the Central Powers of Germany and Austria-Hungary, World War I left Malta relatively untroubled. In one of those ironic twists that litter history, it was the French Navy that came to be invited to use Malta as a base, as the most important units of the Royal Navy, organised as the Grand Fleet, had the North Sea as their main operational area. U-boat activity in the Mediterranean, however, meant that the naval presence there came to be highly cosmopolitan, with forces from Japan, America, Russia, Greece and Italy, as well as Britain, in residence at various

Maxim machine guns on the Victoria Lines. The field carriage mounting conferred mobility and allowed ammunition to be carried in 16 boxes, each containing 250 rounds. Because of their high profile, field carriages were of dubious use when the enemy was equipped with artillery and magazine rifles. They therefore tended to be deployed in colonial warfare scenarios against 'savage' (i.e. poorly armed) enemies. (Photo courtesy of Richard Ellis Ltd.)

times. U-boats, or rather submarines in general, were one of the four main types of weapons and weapons systems that were either invented, or came to fruition, during the Great War. The other three being the tank, poison gas and the aeroplane. The question as it pertained to Malta of course revolved around how the advent of these 'new' weapons would affect the defence of the archipelago and, in the current context, how would the lessons learned in respect of the changes in warfare impact on the fortification of the islands?

As the submarine was a naval weapon and Malta an island, the influence of this weapon was obviously profound in nature. However, since the submarine was primarily a weapon of blockade and not one that would operate close inshore, land-based fortifications were not relevant in defending against submarine attack.

Tanks and armoured warfare presented defensive problems that were not fully realised until the development of machines and tactics especially suited to their characteristics and in any event, in the Maltese context, defence against them was really an extension of amphibious warfare defence. Since early in the 20th century, with the abandonment of the Victoria and Corradino Lines, the defences against this type of attack had moved to the coastline, tank attacks were already expected to be dealt with by the existing defensive arrangements.

The defence against poison gas was largely a matter of personal protective equipment, gas masks and the like, though collective protection could also be applied to certain structures; the various works that comprised the French Maginot Line, for example, were proofed against gas attack. However, since the delivery of gas in the Maltese context would be most likely by air, following the advent of Fascism and the Italian use of it in the 1936 Abyssinian campaign and with the *Regia Aeronautica* within around 20 minutes flying time away, it largely came within the civil and air defence setting. The advent of air power, along with the possession of an efficient air force by Italy, made the defence of Malta in the face of Italian hostility problematical in the extreme. Because of this the survival of Malta then became bound up in the matter of relations with Italy. As the fascist sympathiser Sir Charles Petrie argued:

> Malta ... must be retained even if its value is not what it was in the days before there was aerial warfare, but any such dangers will be reduced

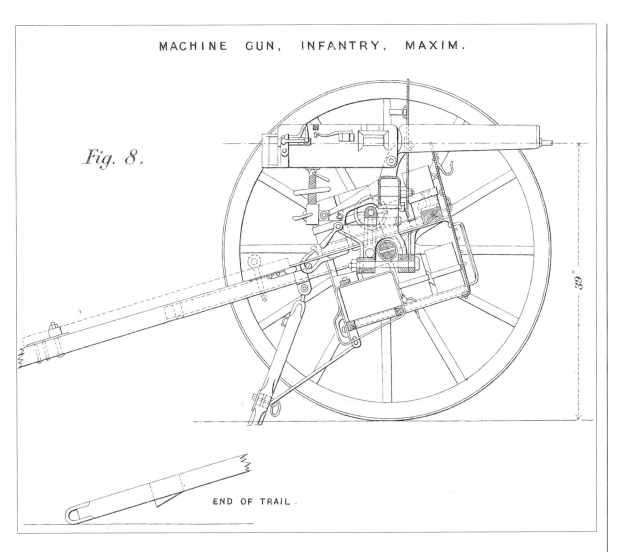

Fig. 8.

39"

END OF TRAIL.

almost to vanishing point if relations between Great Britain and Italy are once restored to the friendly footing on which they stood before the Abyssinian crisis. The future of Malta, as of so much else, depends on such a reconciliation.

Others were not of such a pessimistic outlook, and the constructional details of the last substantial work of coastal fortification undertaken by the British on Malta, Fort Campbell at Tal-Blata between Mellieha Bay and St Paul's Bay, exemplifies the lessons concerning air power. Begun after the 'Abyssinian crisis', in 1937, to house three 152mm guns, it embodied the concept of indirect protection by concealment. The trace of the work was irregular in the extreme in order to mimic the boundaries of fields, whilst machine-gun emplacements and infantry posts, fitted with loopholes for rifles, took up the perimeter defence in place of a ditch with *caponiers* and the like.

Another monument to the presence of air power was constructed just north-west of the village of Ghargur on the Great Fault in 1934/35. Known colloquially as Il-Widna (the ear) this was a pre-radar aircraft early warning system. Correctly, if perhaps less accurately, designated an 'acoustical mirror' it was built in the form of a curved wall measuring some 9m in height and 60m in length. These devices were first developed in Britain in the late 1920s and investigations were undertaken with a view to installing them in overseas

The field carriage was fitted with elevating, traversing and oscillating gears for use in creating a 'beaten zone' impassable to an enemy force. Upper and lower steel shields were fitted for providing protection for the guncrew and the trail shafts could be used to manhandle the device as well as for hitching it to a horse team. Props were used to provide a stable firing base and were swung up and secured when not in use. (Phillips)

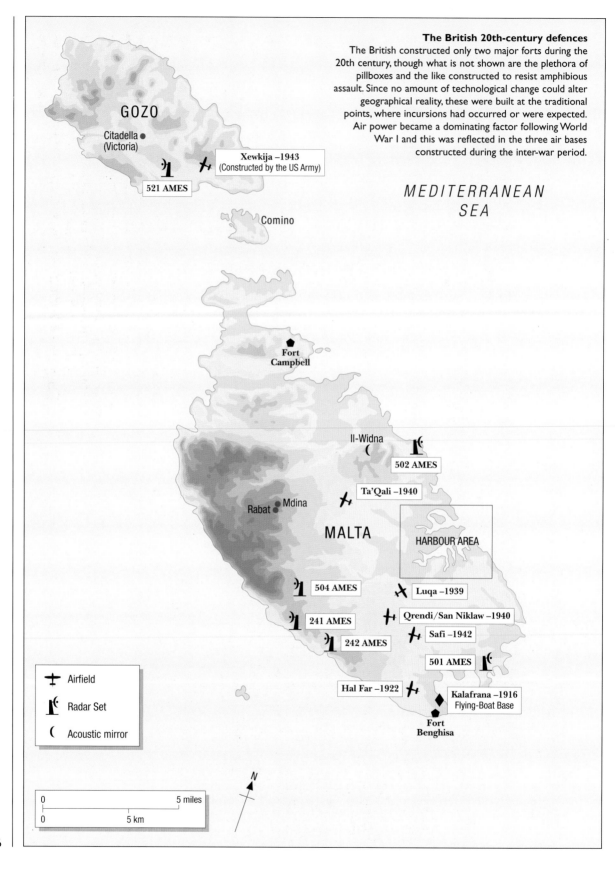

The British 20th-century defences
The British constructed only two major forts during the 20th century, though what is not shown are the plethora of pillboxes and the like constructed to resist amphibious assault. Since no amount of technological change could alter geographical reality, these were built at the traditional points, where incursions had occurred or were expected. Air power became a dominating factor following World War I and this was reflected in the three air bases constructed during the inter-war period.

GOZO

Citadella
(Victoria)

521 AMES

Xewkija –1943
(Constructed by the US Army)

Comino

MEDITERRANEAN SEA

Fort
Campbell

Il-Widna

502 AMES

Ta'Qali –1940

Rabat ● Mdina

MALTA

HARBOUR AREA

504 AMES

Luqa –1939

241 AMES

Qrendi/San Niklaw –1940

242 AMES

Safi –1942

501 AMES

Hal Far –1922

Kalafrana –1916
Flying-Boat Base

Fort
Benghisa

Airfield

Radar Set

Acoustic mirror

0   5 miles
0   5 km

N

Fort Campbell

Situated on the eastern end of Mellieha ridge, Fort Campbell was built in 1937 and was the last major work constructed by the British. It exemplifies how 20th-century technological change impacted on fortification. In the first place it was designed with aircraft very much in mind and was meant to be as invisible as possible from the air. Also, the irregular perimeter wall was made to look rustic like an ordinary field boundary and was punctuated at intervals with machine-gun and rifle posts.

In actual fact, Fort Campbell is something of a misnomer in that it was designed to be more of a battery – accommodating three 152 mm coastal artillery guns. These weapons were the chosen calibre for close defence and had a maximum range of around 23km on their Mk 24 mountings.

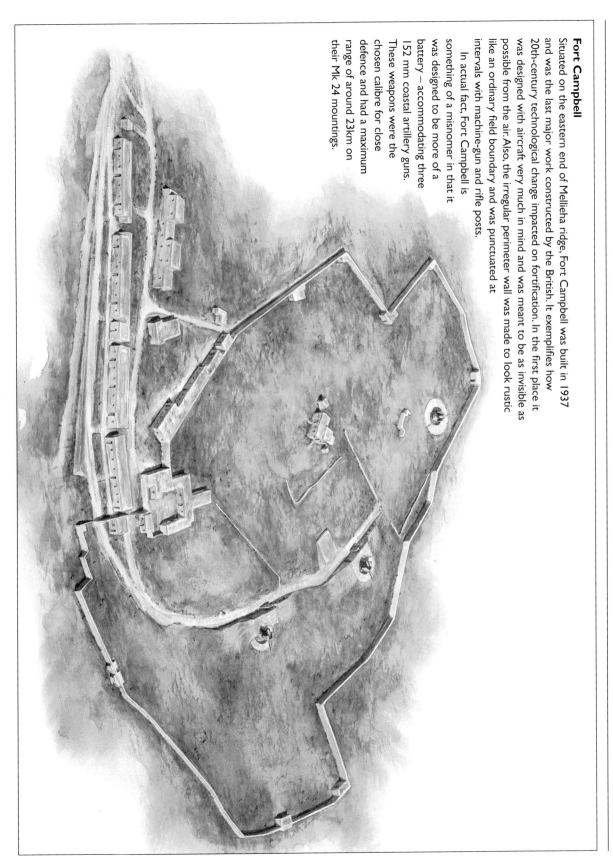

In the summer of 1914 the Imperial German Navy had two warships, the battlecruiser *Goeben* and the light cruiser *Breslau*, based at the Austro-Hungarian port of Pola for deployment in the Mediterranean Sea. When war between Britain and Germany became likely, the *Indomitable* and *Indefatigable*, pictured above in Grand Harbour, required to counter the powerful *Goeben*, were detached from service with the Grand Fleet in the North Sea and sent to Malta.

On 3 August 1914 Germany declared war on France and the German ships, already deployed in the vicinity, attacked French targets in Algeria. Whilst returning eastwards the next day, they encountered the two British batlecruisers on an opposite heading. The two sets of warships passed one another at high speed, before the British reversed course to follow the *Goeben*

and *Breslau*. The Admiralty had issued orders to locate and track the German ships, but not attack until hostilities were officially declared between Britain and Germany.

The German vessels headed east and put on full speed in an effort to shake off the trailing British ships. Despite some trouble with the *Goeben*'s engines, they outran the British, and by nightfall on 4 August just a few hours before Britain declared war, had pulled out of sight of their pursuers. Their destination was Turkey, who 'bought' the vessels and entered the war on the side of the Central Powers.

The failure to engage the *Goeben* and *Breslau*, most definitely not in the glorious tradition of the Royal Navy, was the cause of much anguish, and led to several careers coming to premature and unhappy endings. (Photo courtesy of Richard Ellis Ltd.)

territories such as Hong Kong and Singapore, as well as Malta and Britain itself. They came in three varieties: a 6m and 9m diameter hemispherical bowl-shaped mirror of reinforced concrete and a wall as related above of which only two were constructed, though five were proposed for Malta alone. Il-Widna worked through the reflection and concentration of the sound waves, via the shape of the devices, onto microphones on a forecourt in front of the wall, which was in turn connected to a control room behind the centre of the mirror. This allowed aircraft to be identified from their engine noise at a much greater distance than with the unaided human ear – though only at a maximum range of some 26km according to test reports undertaken at the similar mirror at Denge, Kent, in 1932. However, ranges of between 34km and 60km were achieved at Il-Widna in September 1935.

ABOVE Following the defeat of Imperial Germany, and the internment and eventual scuttling of the High Seas Fleet, the Royal Navy could once again deploy its battle squadrons outside the area of the North Sea. The *Emperor of India*, part of the 4th Battle Squadron, is here pictured in proximity to Fort St Angelo, the HQ of the RN at Malta. In accordance with naval tradition this venerable work was named HMS *St Angelo*, with a spell between 1912 and 1933 as HMS *Egmont*, whilst fulfilling this function. (Photo courtesy of Richard Ellis Ltd.)

BELOW Il-Widna (the ear) represented an attempt to deal with the difficulty of gaining warning of air attack. This was a technological blind-alley as it was unable to establish range and could only give about 5 minutes warning of an aircraft approaching at 500km/h. Sonic direction finding was superseded by radio direction finding and ranging – radar. (Photo by Joe Sammut from *The Victoria Lines*)

World War II and the second siege – 1939–45

The strategic position of Malta during World War II with relation to Italy can be compared with its position during the early days of the Knights. In the 16th century it had disrupted the Ottoman's east–west communications, it now threatened those of Italy on a north–south axis. Or at least potentially, because two conditions had to pertain before the threat could become a reality. Firstly, there had to be sufficient power, both offensive and defensive, to carry out such a policy, and there had to be a requirement for that policy to be activated – in other words a state of war between Britain and Italy.

For Britain, war with Germany came on 3 September 1939 and, as one observer noted, just prior to that 'Malta was denuded of most naval forces'. This was because the Royal Navy had decamped to Alexandria in Egypt, which, by the Anglo–Egyptian treaty of 1936, Britain gained the use of as a naval base. Alexandria was about 1,300km east of Malta, and about 1,600km farther west stood the fortress of Gibraltar, which controlled entry to and from the Atlantic. Basing the fleet at Alexandria also helped to reinforce British control of the Suez Canal and thus made it impossible for the Italians to reinforce and supply their East African forces in Abyssinian and Eritrea by sea. However, in the case of a war with Italy this strategy of trading space for protection would be of little use in securing communications between Britain and Egypt, or severing them between Italy and its African territory. In the event of war with Italy, British strategy had to be dictated by these necessities and whatever the tactical problems might be, it would be a strategic necessity to exploit Malta's commanding position, augmented by the presence of powerful French naval units in the western Mediterranean and a Royal Navy presence at Gibraltar.

Italy did declare war on Britain and France, but not until 10 June 1940, when Germany's military forces had shattered their French and British counterparts, and just 11 days before the French government accepted terms from Hitler. A powerful Allied navy had been removed from the equation, whilst one almost as strong had been added on the other side, along with a modern and experienced air force. Britain's Mediterranean position, with all that implied for Malta, looked bleak. One of the first actions of the Italians was to cut two of the five cables between Gibraltar and Malta, with the rest being severed shortly afterwards. Malta was then without direct cable communication with London and remained so until Italy had been defeated. However, communication was maintained because three of the five cables between Malta and Alexandria continued to function right through the war.

The day after the declaration of war, at 0700hrs ten Italian aircraft approached Malta at about 4,000m and were engaged by the airborne and ground defences; antiquated Gladiator fighters, anti-aircraft guns from positions near the Grand Harbour and dockyard defence batteries. There were a few minor naval units in Grand Harbour and these added to the defensive fire. This raid was to be the first of eight that day and between 11 June and the end of 1940 there were to be over 100 air raids of varying strengths by the *Regia Aeronautica*, supplemented thereafter by the *Luftwaffe*. This was done with a view to neutralising Malta as a base from which offensive operations against communications with North Africa could be mounted; a matter that became pressing following British military successes against Italian forces there and the dispatch of the German Afrika Korps to support them. British and Commonwealth forces under Wavell had begun an offensive into Italian territory on 9 December 1940 and Tobruk and Dema were captured in January.

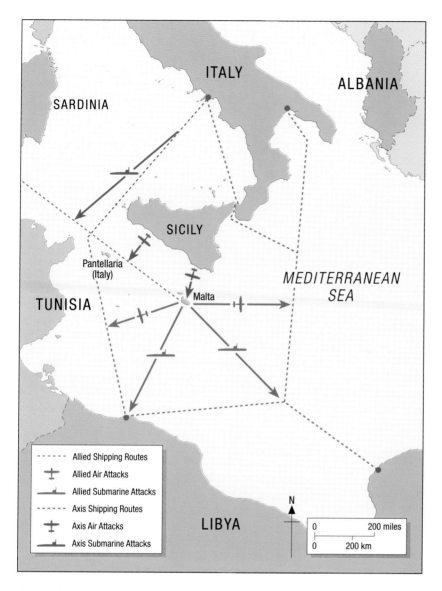

Allied and Axis lines of communication. Following the acquisition of a North African empire in the early years of the 20th century, Italian north–south communications with Libya were potentially threatened by British possession of Malta. This potential was realised following the outbreak of hostilities between Italy and Britain in 1940. The opposite was also true as British and Allied communications with Malta were at peril due to Italian and Axis interdiction. Shown here are the salient elements of this two-way battle of attrition conducted on both sides by sea and air. The *matériel* advantage lay with the Allies, who could draw on neutral shipping and US industrial resources.

On 6 February Benghazi was entered, but the offensive was then brought to a halt by the political decision to withdraw forces to Greece. Driven by these British successes the decision was taken to send a German armoured contingent to Libya, but the Germans knew that forces at Malta threatened their ability to send and maintain these reinforcements. To send Rommel's Afrika Korps without mitigating British abilities to interdict communications by sea would be a hazardous enterprise. Malta was the key and both sides saw clearly enough that the issue would depend on the outcome of the campaign to neutralise Malta as an effective offensive base, however, the offensive operations against Axis shipping had not started successfully. This is shown by the fact that from February through to March 1941, a German armoured division and half a million tons of their equipment were carried across the central Mediterranean using some 100 transport vessels, some 220,000 tonnes of shipping, of which only six, around 20,000 tonnes, were sunk.

It has previously been argued that the construction of fortified areas, such as the Maltese archipelago might be termed, has a dual purpose: that of providing defensive protection and also forming a secure base from which offensive operations may be carried out. The offensive operations against Axis shipping

By May 1941 the public around the harbour area were encouraged to dig into the rock beneath the ancient fortifications to form extempore air-raid shelters. (Courtesy of Progress Press Ltd. Malta)

were carried out during World War II by both submarine and plane and as the Axis codes were compromised by Bletchley Park, their operations began to take an increasing toll. It was information from Bletchley that led to probably the single greatest operation against the Axis lines of communication, when it was learned that three Italian liners were due to sail from Taranto to Tripoli packed with German troops. That information was received on 17 September 1941 and by the following early morning British submarines were waiting off the coast of Libya, where experience had shown the Italian convoys made their landfall. The action was brilliantly successful, with two liners sunk, the 20,000-tonne sisters *Oceania* and *Neptunia*, and some 5,000 German troops drowned. However, even before this action the disruption and losses on the supply routes to North Africa had caused great concern to the Axis. The Chief of the German Naval Staff in Italy had pointed this out on 9 September, warning that the most dangerous British forces in the Mediterranean were the submarines, especially those operating from Malta, which claimed 11 ships of over 60,000 tonnes during that month. The problem with continuing losses on such a scale was that, unlike the Allies engaged in the Battle of the Atlantic, Italy could neither draw on neutral shipping, nor build fast enough to replace the tonnage destroyed. In 1936 J. F. C. Fuller had articulated the iron principle that 'supply is the foundation of strategy, and … the velocity of an … operation is in proportion to its maintenance' and the Axis forces in North Africa were to find their 'velocity' reduced to zero, due in large part to the offensive operations conducted from the fortified island of Malta. As in the Atlantic, the maritime struggle in the Mediterranean and the consequent result of the military campaigns in North Africa turned on supply. This is an important point: Malta was not attacked and besieged simply because it was there, but because of the vital contribution it was making to the defeat of Axis power.

The Axis powers were of course well aware of the depredations being inflicted by forces based on Malta. They sought to 'restrain', in the words of the Maltese author Joseph Attard, 'the wolf that was eating 80 per cent' of the supplies sent to North Africa. This 'restraint' was to take a form somewhat similar to one that had been mooted previously in relation to Britain itself; the island would be invaded, but first the defences, particularly the air defences, would be suppressed by air attack before Operation Herkules, as the invasion project came to be called, was implemented.

Operation Herkules

The invasion of Malta was to be accomplished by a combination of airborne and amphibious attacks, and was scheduled for July/August 1942. The implementation of the plan was contingent upon two things: the effective suppression of the air defences by the *Luftwaffe* and *Regia Aeronautica*, and success in the North African campaign from where forces for the operation were to be drawn. Militarily, these were to consist of one brigade-strength force of German paratroops and one complete Italian airborne division for the initial assault. This combined force, numbering some 30,000, was equivalent to the whole Malta garrison. The air component to deliver them was to comprise over 500 troop-carrying aircraft, together with roughly the same number of gliders. To escort this assault force the *Luftwaffe* and *Regia Aeronautica* would each provide over 200 fighters and, if required, a further 600 bomber and ground-assault aircraft were available to suppress the defences.

Virtually the whole *Regia Marina* was to sortie in support, with five battleships, four heavy cruisers, 21 destroyers, 14 submarines as well as light forces and landing-craft. Some 70,000 troops were scheduled for the amphibious assault, comprising an Italian infantry division supported by a German tank regiment with a German mountain division in reserve. Ominously for the defenders, the command of the assaulting forces was assigned to General Kurt Student, who had successfully conquered Crete using similar methods. However, neither the Italian nor German forces had much experience in amphibious warfare, though plenty in the airborne variety, at least on the German side. Nevertheless, Student's plan was accepted by Axis commanders at a conference that included representatives of the Imperial Japanese Navy and Army, both organisations that had extensive expertise in the matter.

Operation Herkules was to proceed in four phases with the object of capturing Valletta, for once that object was achieved it was considered that organised resistance would cease. Student largely concurred with de la Valette in his strategic insight of 1565 that St Elmo and, by extension, the city that bore de la Valette's name, formed the 'key to Malta'.

That Operation Herkules was never attempted is a matter of fact and why this was so is also fairly clear. The ultimate driving force behind Axis strategic decision-making was Adolf Hitler and Germany's Führer was strategist enough

Situated just inside the city gate, the historic Valetta opera house was destroyed during April 1942. Today, it remains much as depicted here as a reminder of the Second Siege. (Courtesy of Progress Press Ltd. Malta)

OPPOSITE Operation Herkules. The operation to capture Malta was supposed to commence with an airdrop, at reinforced battalion strength, securing the coastline between Wied iz-Zurrieq and Ghar Lapsi. This assault force was to be dispatched in gliders at dawn and approach the south coast of Malta from the west, with the aim of establishing a bridgehead and, if possible, capturing the airfield close by at Hal Far. Close air support would be provided by the 'flying artillery' of the *Luftwaffe* and *Regia Aeronautica*.

With the bridgehead secured, the second phase was to commence with the amphibious landing onto the beaches of elements of *La Spezia* and the panzer regiment. Simultaneously, the entire remaining parachute complement of the force was to drop in the area south of the twin cities of Mdina/Rabat, moving on to capture them as soon as possible.

The third phase would begin with the force in the bridgehead striking eastwards with the object of either consolidating, or indeed capturing if this had not been achieved, Hal Far airfield and taking the smaller strip at Safi. The ultimate objective of this thrust was the harbour at Birzebuggar. In co-ordination with this manoeuvre, the paratroops were to spread out from the Mdina/Rabat area and move north-east towards Ta'Qali and south-east to Luqa airfield to prevent Allied use of the airfields. The reserve mountain division could be airlifted into Hal Far and Safi airfields, provided of course that they had been captured.

Phase four was to start with the remaining elements of *La Spezia* landing at Birzebuggar and then all components were to advance on Valletta. *La Spezia* and the armour from the south, whilst the airborne troops were to strike from the west towards Sliema. The intention was for these forces to join up at Floriana and cut off Valletta. Once Valletta was taken the operation was considered to be over.

RIGHT The steadfastness of the defenders of Malta, whether military or civilian, in the face of all enemy efforts short of actual invasion was recognised by the award of the George Cross to the islands. On Sunday 13 September 1942 Viscount Gort, the Governor of Malta and representative of King George VI, presented the Maltese Chief Justice, Sir George Borg, representing the island and people of Malta, with the medal at a ceremony in Palace Square, Valletta. (Courtesy of Progress Press Ltd. Malta)

to know that the war would be decided on the Eastern Front. He was, however, sentimental enough to allow essentially secondary operations in support of his Italian ally to bleed away forces. When these forces achieved success in North Africa then he obviously wished to exploit it. This was particularly so when the prospect of Axis forces in the Middle East linking up with those in the Caucasus became realistic. This perception hardened after 21 June 1942 when Tobruk, together with 33,000 prisoners and a huge amount of booty, was captured and within days Alexandria was threatened. Churchill later wrote that this news was one of the 'heaviest blows' that he could recall. Strategically, carrying out Operation Herkules required shutting down an ostensibly successful advance in order to devote substantial forces to an already, if temporarily, neutralised communications threat. This would, from Hitler's perspective, have been an unsound operation. Tactically, there were also doubts as to the soundness of the plan. Hitler, though he had decreed on 2 December 1941 that it was 'particularly important to suppress Malta' had nevertheless pronounced himself sceptical of future massed airborne drops after the capture of Crete. He was also doubtful of the stamina of the *Regia Marina*, fearing that they would hesitate to hazard their major units in a showdown with Britain's fleet.

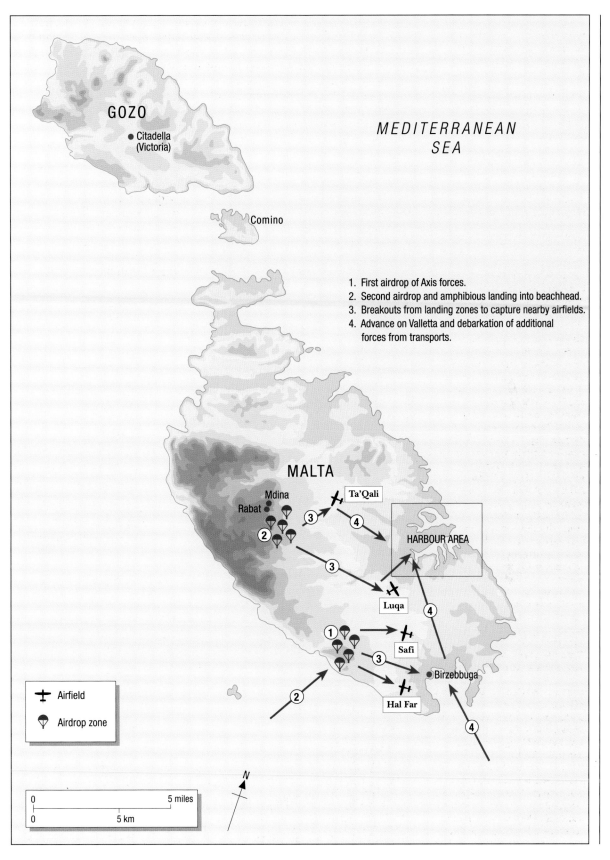

GOZO

● Citadella
(Victoria)

Comino

MEDITERRANEAN
SEA

1. First airdrop of Axis forces.
2. Second airdrop and amphibious landing into beachhead.
3. Breakouts from landing zones to capture nearby airfields.
4. Advance on Valletta and debarkation of additional
   forces from transports.

MALTA

Mdina

Rabat

Ta'Qali

HARBOUR AREA

Luqa

Safi

● Birzebbuga

Hal Far

✈ Airfield

🪂 Airdrop zone

0   5 miles
0   5 km

N

That the strategic decision was a miscalculation of major proportions was only later realised when the Axis supply position in North Africa became perilous in the extreme following the battle of El Alamein, Operation Torch and the re-emergence of Malta as a base for offensive operations. Tactically it can be argued that Hitler's errors of judgement were equally as grave. The defences against such an operation as Herkules are considered below, but in one respect he was totally mistaken: the Royal Navy in the Mediterranean had been massively depleted by the end of 1941, particularly with regard to heavy units. If the Italian Navy had sortied in force, a fleet action was unlikely. Crucially, neither Hitler nor the Italians knew this.

Air power and the demise of fortification as a military science

The several centuries of fortification to which Malta had been subject had all had the object of making the island as impervious to invasion as possible. Air power, in the form it had evolved into in the 1940s, had rendered the science of fortification, and all previous systems associated with it, useless. Taking warfare into the air caused enormous problems for the science of fortification. Of the two basic elements of fortification, protection and obstacle, the former could certainly be achieved by the construction of shelters and the like offering direct protection. Obstacle, however, was problematic in the extreme, largely confined to barrage balloons. Indirect protection could also be achieved by concealment and camouflage, but, just as the value of direct protection had always been reduced if the defenders had to expose themselves to return fire, in order to counter air attack the defence had to be active as well as passive. In other words, visible and obvious airfields for airborne defences, and, somewhat less visible and obvious, batteries of anti-aircraft artillery were required. To use Mao's analogy, the spear had finally achieved ascendancy over the shield.

At the time of the outbreak of war in 1939 there were three airfields existing or under construction on the island: Hal Far (Fleet Air Arm), Luqa (Bomber Command) and Ta Qali (Fighter Command), in addition there was a seaplane base at Kalafrana. Construction was begun in 1940 of a satellite airfield close to Luqa, Qrendi-San Niklaw, and Safi, a narrow, rock-hewn landing strip, was started in 1941. However, demands from other theatres, compounded by a reluctance to send scarce resources to a location perceived as extremely vulnerable, meant that Malta's airborne defences were somewhat minimalist. However, one crucial component was cutting edge, for in March 1939 Malta received one of the first three radar sets to leave Britain. Capable of plotting high-flying aircraft this was, for security reasons, designated 241 AMES (Air Ministry Experimental Station) and located at Dingli Cliffs. In June 1940 a second station capable of locating and plotting medium- and low-flying aircraft, 242 AMES, was set up at Ghar Lapsi, and the ground-based defences at that time consisted of 34 heavy and eight light anti-aircraft guns, as well as 24 searchlights. By mid-1941 three more radar units were operational: 501 AMES at Tas Silg, 502 AMES at Madliena and 504 AMES also at Dingli. A GCI (Ground Control Interception) station was located near Salina Bay for controlling and coordinating the fighter defence. Two more radar stations came into operation during February 1942 and the defences were further augmented by intelligence-gathering units, which monitored the tactical communications of the Germans and Italians. On the strategic level, relevant enemy signals were received and distributed by a Special Liaison Unit, based at the War HQ in Valletta, which was in receipt of 'Ultra' intelligence decrypted at Bletchley Park in Britain. Crucially then, had Herkules been attempted, it is probable that the defenders would have had advanced warning, a potentially formidable advantage. The physical defences were also formidable.

Immediately prior to the outbreak of war an invasion force landing in the north of the island had been considered the most likely eventuality, hence a large number of pillboxes and other fixed defences had been constructed there, particularly around and along the Marfa Ridge and around the bays of Mellieha and St Paul's. Subsequently, many more were built on the southern coast, particularly around Marsaxlokk Bay, which was where the main landings were planned. However, by resorting to air-landed forces the invaders intended to bypass these and take them in the rear. Malta was also well equipped with anti-aircraft batteries and undoubtedly all available air and naval forces would have been deployed. In short, whilst Herkules was undoubtedly an operation conceived on the grand scale, it would have been hazardous and its likely success or failure must remain within the sphere of the wargamer and armchair general.

The steadfastness of the defenders of Malta, whether military or civilian, in the face of all enemy efforts short of actual invasion was recognised by the award of the George Cross to the islands. The fruits of this defiance were realised the following year when on 10 July 1943 Operation Husky, the invasion of Sicily, commenced. On the 25th Benito Mussolini was deposed by the Fascist Grand Council and, on 8 September, the day after the Allies crossed the Straits of Messina into mainland Italy and the day before they landed at Salerno, the terms of their armistice with Italy were announced – 378 years to the day after the Ottoman forces evacuated Malta following the first Great Siege. The ultimate outcome is perhaps best expressed in the official communication sent to the Permanent Secretary to the Admiralty by the C-in-C Mediterranean dated 11 September 1943: 'Be pleased to inform Their Lordships that the Italian battle fleet now lies under the guns of the fortress of Malta.'

The Second Siege, though very different from its predecessor, had resulted in a victory of incalculably greater proportions. That this was so was due in no small degree to a similar factor: in the face of apparently insuperable odds, the defenders, both civilian and military, had refused to give way.

The Lippija Tower, one of the smaller types constructed between 1636 and 1657 alongside a World War II pillbox. (Photo by Joe Sammut from *The Victoria Lines*)

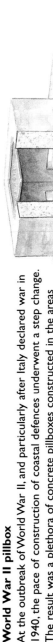

World War II pillbox

At the outbreak of World War II, and particularly after Italy declared war in 1940, the pace of construction of coastal defences underwent a step change. The result was a plethora of concrete pillboxes constructed in the areas threatened by amphibious landings. These 'hostilities' pillboxes went through three design phases before arriving at the one depicted, though they were all fundamentally similar and had identical tactical purposes: providing a secure emplacement for machine guns. They were far more than just 20th-century versions of the Knights' watchtowers and were arranged to channel attackers into 'killing zones'.

The Vickers heavy machine gun is depicted on a 'swinging arm' mount, which could be locked into position for delivering fire on specific, pre-determined points. Each gun needed two men, a gunner and loader, whilst an observer situated in the observation turret would direct the fire. Loopholes in the walls were provided for rifle fire, but if an enemy appeared to be close enough to launch grenade or flame-thrower attacks, the position would be abandoned. Hits from medium artillery would also have been fatal, given that the roof was only some 381mm thick, and the walls about 254mm. No ventilation facilities were provided, and so protection against gas attack would have to come from gas masks.

Malta today

The Maltese archipelago became independent in 1964 and a republic in 1974. Thus, for the first time, the Maltese people gained control of their own destiny. Post-war changes, both in geo-politics and weapons technology, means that the strategic position of Malta has declined somewhat in importance. Probably its last major contribution to naval enterprise came in 1956, when it was the base from which the combined Anglo-French fleet launched their politically disastrous operations against Egypt. The repercussions of this operation confirmed the demise of European political and military strategic independence.

Be that as it may, Malta's many centuries of strategic importance have left it with a military-archaeological legacy that is probably unique, for few places elsewhere on the globe can boast such a variety of fortifications in such a small area. Happily, the great majority have survived and can be seen to this day, particularly around Valletta and the harbour area, parts of which are a World Heritage Site. Many of the cannon that were inherited by the British were later utilised as bollards by being sunk muzzle-first, and these can still be seen at various places around the periphery of Grand Harbour. There are many operators offering boat trips around the harbour area and these are well worth undertaking, if only to marvel at the magnitude of the work that went into constructing the formidable fortifications. Napoleon Bonaparte's brief visit is commemorated by a plaque on the wall of the Post Office in Merchants' Street, Valletta. This building was formerly the Parisio Palace, where he stayed for one eventful week.

The National War Museum is located at Fort St Elmo, and as its handbook states:

> The choice of Fort St Elmo as the location for the National War Museum was a most appropriate one. There are few places in Valletta that can claim greater fame than this old Fortress. The epic defence of the Fort against the invading Turks in the Great Siege of 1565 provides one of the brightest chapters in Malta's history.

The exhibits in the museum however relate mainly to the WWII period – the Second Siege – and range from General Eisenhower's Jeep – 'Husky' after the invasion of Sicily – to the George Cross inscribed 'To the Island of Malta 15 April 1942'. There is also an illuminated scroll from President Franklin D. Roosevelt, saluting 'The Island of Malta, its people and defenders', dated 7 December 1943 – the second anniversary of America's entry into World War II. Visitors to Fort St Elmo can also witness historical re-enactments, which are held throughout the year. Around 90 officers and men-at-arms in period costumes perform a series of military drills in the fort, including marching, changing of the guard, manning of posts, orders of the day, musketry and gunnery drill, parade fall-in, presentation of arms and colours. For details of these, and for the opening times of the National War Museum, visitors can contact the National Tourism Organisation Malta on: +356 22 64 05, or fax: +356 22 04 01

The British works, though they are less visually spectacular, remain to a great extent as well, from the largest down to the pillboxes constructed to resist invasion prior to, and during, World War II. A restoration project is underway to reclaim parts of the Victoria Lines from the decay into which they have fallen and a walk along the Great Fault in the footsteps of many centuries of warriors is a rewarding experience.

Getting to Malta is comparatively simple in the age of affordable air travel and as well as charter flights operated as part of package holidays, the national airline, Air Malta, operates flights to and from all the major airports in Europe. The islands are also included in several cruise itineraries and scheduled ferries sail direct from several Mediterranean ports. One of the great advantages for visitors to Malta is the small size of the archipelago and all points are accessible on the excellent bus service.

The official languages are Maltese and English, so English-speaking visitors in particular will find themselves quite at home and all are made very welcome. Maltese summers are very hot, dry and sunny. Cooling sea breezes often mitigate the temperatures in summer, but in spring and autumn a very hot wind from Africa occasionally brings unseasonably high temperatures and humidity. This is known as the sirocco, or, in Maltese, the xlokk.

The Maltese people take advantage of a siesta, so that shops are normally open between 0900hrs and 1300hrs and between 1600hrs and 1900hrs. However, in tourist areas many shops remain open till 2200hrs. Shops are normally closed on Sundays and Public Holidays, of which there are no fewer than 14.

The tap water is safe to drink and Malta has an excellent health service. Hospitals are modern and supported by a regional network of health centres and there are reciprocal health agreements with Australia and the United Kingdom. Nationals of these countries, if staying for no more than a month, are entitled to free medical and hospital care.

Politically, the Maltese Republic is a European-style liberal democracy with all the associated freedoms. Most Maltese adhere to the Catholic faith, but there are Anglican, Church of Scotland, Greek Orthodox, Jewish, Methodist and Muslim communities.

The Malta of today is a peaceful and hospitable place, with the depredations of corsairs and Fascists long since ceased. However, in certain portions, particularly St Paul's Bay and Qawra, there has been an infestation of timeshare touts who seem to have similarly predatory aims.

It is still possible to stand upon the very same ramparts as those who watched for the Ottomans over the centuries, and the Fascist enemy more recently. With a little concentration, and perhaps somewhat more imagination, it is possible to envisage what it must have been like to man those defences against an omnipresent threat.

Glossary

barbette a platform, whether raised or not, on which guns are mounted to fire over a parapet. Pieces so mounted are said to be *en barbette*.

bastion a bastion projected outwards from the main walls of a defended area, the *enceinte*, with the object of allowing the defenders to see and subject to cross, or enfilading, fire, any attacking force. It comprised two faces, coming together to form a point, two flanks, and a gorge, or neck, where it joined the main work. Bastions were also constructed at the junction of two walls meeting at obtuse angles, thus offering enfilading fire down both walls.

bonnet a small counterguard in front of the salient angle of a ravelin.

caponier a sheltered defensible passage across the ditch of a fort to the outerworks. Also a work within the ditch, used to provide flanking fire.

casemate a chamber built in the thickness of the ramparts or *cavalier* and used as a barrack or gun position firing through embrasures.

cavalier a work built above a bastion or curtain wall, and so designed as to command the surrounding ground with artillery, usually mounted in casemates. Fort St Elmo, as originally constructed, had two *cavaliers*, one being massive and detached. The reconstruction featured an even larger type on the site of the original detached version, though brought within the *enceinte* of the fort with the addition of curtain walls. The original plan for the construction of the Valletta defences featured no less than nine *cavaliers* behind bastions. In the event only two were constructed.

counterguard a large outerwork, open at the gorge, designed to protect the faces of bastions and ravelins.

counterscarp the outer wall of the ditch facing the ramparts.

counterscarp gallery a casemate within the counterscarp situated at the corners to provide flanking fire along the ditch.

covered way or **covertway** a path on top of the counterscarp, protected by a parapet formed from the crest of the glacis, where the defending troops could manoeuvre. An enlarged area of the covered way, where a body of troops might assemble, was known as a place of arms.

crowned hornwork a hornwork protected further by a crownwork. The Floriana Lines featured a crowned hornwork, further enhanced with a ravelin in front of one of the curtain wall of the crownwork.

crownwork an outerwork, projected ahead of the main work in order to cover an area considered vulnerable. It consisted of a central bastion and two demi-bastions connected with short curtain walls. The name derived from the appearance of the trace, or plan view, of the arrangement.

demi-bastion a half-bastion with one face and one or two flanks.

detached *lunette* an advanced work in the form of a *lunette* connected to the covered way by a *caponier*. Detached *lunettes* featured in the Floriana Lines.

ditch a dry trench outside a fortified work, usually rock hewn, to obstruct direct assault on the main walls.

drop-ditch a ditch to protect a *caponier*.

embrasure an opening cut in the parapet through which a gun could be fired without exposing the guncrew, normally wider at the front than at the rear.

entrenched bastion a bastion with an entrenchment built into its gorge.

glacis the sloping ground in front of a fortress spanning from the top of the parapet of the covertway down until it reaches the open country, cleared of all obstacles to bring an advancing enemy into the direct line of fire.

hornwork an outerwork consisting of a front of two demi-bastions joined by a short curtain wall, the name deriving from the appearance in plan.

lunette a large outerwork rather like a detached bastion. *Lunettes* featured in the Floriana Lines.

neck of bastion also known as the gorge of the bastion.

openwork any work not protected by a parapet at the gorge.

orillon a shoulder on a bastion where it joins the curtain wall. Fort St Elmo, both originally and as reconstructed, featured *orillons* on its landward-facing bastions.

ravelin a work shaped like a spearhead, which was constructed in front of a curtain wall, and could be attached or detached. Ravelins featured in the defensive *enceintes* of Fort Manoel, Fort Ricasoli, and the Floriana Lines.

redan a triangular extension from the curtain. Redans were features of the coastal and inland entrenchments.

scarp or **escarp** the main wall of a defensive work forming the inner side of the ditch, and facing outwards towards the counterscarp. The length of a rampart between two bastions was also referred to as a curtain.

tenaille a small outerwork, basically a wall, placed inside the ditch between two adjoining bastions, and designed to protect the curtain wall. It was usually detached but sometimes linked to the flanks or shoulders of adjoining bastions. *Tennailles* were constructed at Fort Ricasoli and the Floriana Lines.

terraplein the material forming the body of a rampart behind a parapet. Sometimes formed from packed earth or rubble excavated during the digging of the ditch.

Bibliography

Books

The works of Attard, Bradford, Elliott, Pickles, Shores *et al.*, Spiteri and Zammit are particularly recommended, as is the *National War Museum Official Guide*.

Attard, Joseph, *The Battle of Malta* (London: Hamlyn, 1982)

Bono, Emilio de, *Anno XIII: The Conquest of an Empire* (London: Cresset, 1937)

Bradford, Ernle, *The Great Siege: Malta 1565* (London: Hodder, 1961)

Clarke, Sir George Sydenham, *Fortification: It's Past Achievements, Recent Developments, And Future Progress* (London: Beaufort Publishing, 1890 & 1907)

The Encyclopaedia Britannica. 14th Edition (London, 1929)

Elliott Peter, *The Cross and the Ensign: A Naval History of Malta 1798–1979* (London: P. Stephens, 1980)

Fuller, J. F. C., *The First of the League Wars* (London: Eyre & Spottiswoode, 1936)

Gibbon, Edward, *The History of the Decline and Fall of the Roman Empire* (London: J. B. Bury, 1788)

Gilbert, Martin, *Winston S. Churchill: Road to Victory 1941–1945* (London: Houghton Mifflin, 1986)

National War Museum Official Guide (Available only from the Museum)

Hill, Richard, *War at Sea in the Ironclad Age* (London: Weidenfeld & Nicholson, 2000)

Inalcik, Halil, *The Ottoman Empire. The Classical Age 1300–1600* (London: Weidenfeld & Nicholson, 1973)

Jane, Fred T., *The British Battle Fleet: Its Inception And Growth Throughout The Centuries* (London: Conway Classics, 1912)

Keyes, Admiral of the Fleet The Lord, *Amphibious Warfare and Combined Operations* (Cambridge: Cambridge University Press, 1943)

Petrie, Sir Charles, *Lords of the Inland Sea: A Study of the Mediterranean Powers* (London, 1937)

Philips, G., *Text Book on Fortification Etc.*, (London: Pardon & Sons, 1899)

Pickles, Tim, Campaign 50: *Malta 1565: Last Battle of the Crusades* (Oxford: Osprey, 1998)

Roskill, Stephen, *The Navy at War 1939–1945* (London: HMSO, 1954–61)

Scarth, Richard N., *Echoes From the Sky* (Hythe Civic Society, 1999)

Shores, Christopher, and Cull, Brian, with Malizia, Nicola, *Malta: The Hurricane Years. 1940–41* (London: Grub Street, 1987)

Shores, Christopher, and Cull, Brian, with Malizia, Nicola, *Malta: The Spitfire Year. 1942* (London: Grub Street, 1991)

Spiteri, Stephen C., *British Military Architecture in Malta* (Malta, 1996)

Spiteri, Stephen C., *Fortresses of the Knights* (Malta: Publishers Enterprise Group, 2001)

Zammit, Ray Cachia (Ed), *The Victoria Lines* (Malta: Progress Press, 1996)

Websites

www.fortressexplorer.org (Stephen C. Spiteri's website)

The view of the south-west turret of the Red Tower, also known as St Agatha's Tower, clearly shows the splayed merlons added to the design for decorative or, as some have argued, deterrent effect. The tower, recently restored and open to the public, is worth a visit for its magnificent views if nothing else. (Courtesy of P. Evans)

Index

Figures in **bold** refer to illustrations